THE BIG QUESTIONS OF LIFE

THE BIG QUESTIONS OF LIFE

OM SWAMI

os.me

First published in India by HarperCollins
Publishers in 2019
Worldwide rights: Om Swami Meditations, Inc.

www.os.me

ISBN: 978-93-5357-719-3

CONTENTS

I SAMSARA

II LONELINESS

III SELF

IV AWAKENING

I
SAMSARA

THE ABC OF LIFE

Is there no way out of the suffering this life sometimes seems to be?

'Swamiji,' my father said to me the other day, 'life has taught me that one must go through one's journey alone.'

He was a bit unsettled, even distraught, as he had recently fallen prey to a fraudulent phone call telling him that his bank card had been blocked. (Mis)leading him through a series of steps, the caller managed to extract his bank details and in under just two minutes, spent my parents' entire one month's pension on various websites. The bank concluded that it was my father's negligence that was behind this disaster, for he'd shared the transaction password with the caller. Understandably, the police couldn't do much because the call was traced to another state in India.

In the larger scheme of things, it's nothing: to lose one month's worth of pension when you've been earning for more than four decades. But, as is the way of loss, it is rarely about the absolute nature of the loss itself or its magnitude, and more about how victimized we feel. An unexpected, undesirable incident can catch even the wisest completely off-guard. It took my father more than two weeks to come to terms with the fact that he was tricked. My mother, on the other hand, was cool as the winter breeze and didn't so much as even blink at this monetary loss.

Two people under the same roof, bearing the same loss, are affected differently. What a beautiful and intriguing world we live in.

'I've seen,' Father added, recounting his difficult childhood, 'that no one is there when you are suffering. Only your grit and God's grace help a person sail through. No one else can help.'

I knew where he was coming from, because many people I meet feel utterly lonely when they are down. They are usually not alone, but even with all the help around, loneliness seems to seep in like water through cracks – cracks in our consciousness, and in our understanding of ourselves and our view of life. That's why the Buddha deemed *samyaka dṛṣṭi* (right view of life) as one of the most important elements of self-realization. Krishna, too, repeatedly reminds Arjuna about the impermanent nature of everything and that one must navigate through the duality of life with courage.

mātrā-sparśhāstu kaunteya śhītoṣhṇa-sukha-duḥkha-dāḥ…
(Bhagavad Gita 2.14)

Forget things, he goes on to say, one day, even all the people you love or hate, won't be in your life or you in theirs (*avyaktādīni bhūtāni vyakta-madhyāni bhārata* ... [Bhagavad Gita 2.28]). So, what are you brooding over? Loss in (and of) life is not a question of if, but when. Whatever we are attached to or hold dear in our hearts, losing it is only a matter of time. It is inevitable.

'Of course,' I said to my father, 'no one can partake of our suffering, I agree. It's a personal matter. Just like no one else will feel full if *you* have a hearty meal, or hungry, if *you* are deprived of one.'

He nodded, relieved that I, whom he also looks upon as his guru, validated his view.

'However,' I continued, 'they *can* share your loss, they *can* share your pain. You may not pass on the fulfilment of a good meal but you *can* share your food with them. Thereafter, whether they feel full or foul is up to them. And, that's what suffering is: it is not what is happening to us but how we see what is happening to us. It is not the actual situation but our interpretation of it that then governs our feelings. Change the interpretation and feelings change on their own.'

You can't change your feelings by just wanting to change them, no matter how desperate or strong-willed you may be. You need to find out what is evoking these emotions in you. Go to the source. It could be an incident or a set of incidents, certain people, and so on. Then ask yourself if you wish to feel differently. If so, begin with the assumption that nothing or no one else is going to change. They are where they always have been, they are exactly where they are supposed to be. Develop a broader view, distract yourself positively, look at the brighter side, practise loving-kindness towards yourself and others, and gradually, your perspective will begin to shift. When it does, everything else will shift with it.

> Once the Buddha was confronted by a monster called Suciloma, whose name translates as 'Needle-hair'. He was a prototype punk with needles for hair! He wanted to find out if the Buddha was really enlightened. So, he sat next to the Buddha and leaned towards him to prick him, but the Buddha leaned away.
>
> 'Aha!' said Needle-hair. 'You don't like pain. You're not really enlightened. An enlightened person would maintain equanimity no matter what. He wouldn't have any likes or dislikes.'
>
> The Buddha said, 'Don't be stupid. There are things that are going to cause problems for my body. It's going to hurt it and make it unhealthy' (SN 10:53).[1]
>
> This is just common sense. You don't step on snakes, you don't run into fires, and you don't allow needles to poke you. You move away. It's common sense, not attachment.
>
> That's loving-kindness toward your body: keeping it healthy, keeping it safe.[2]

Often blinded by our experiences, conditioning, and set in our ways, though, that's exactly what we do: we step on snakes, run into fire and allow needles to poke us. Snakes of attachments, fire of desires, and needles of jealousy and covetousness. They bite, burn and hurt. We call it suffering and we think that this is the way of life. We mistake our pain for our suffering. We have little control over the former, but the latter is almost entirely in our hands. We can take things in our stride or be tossed into the tide. This choice, we must remember, is in our hands. At all times.

~

A man went to a pizzeria and ordered a large whole-wheat pizza with a diet Coke.

'Should I cut it into six slices or ten?' the owner asked.

'Ten! Ten!' the man winced. 'Someone's trying to lose weight here! Cut it into six!'

It's the same life; if you want it all to yourself, then whether you divide it in six or ten, it doesn't matter. As I wrote in *Mind Full to Mindful*, 'Nothing matters. Eventually.' The sooner you realize this, the quicker conflicts or challenges will stop bothering you.

Pain is inevitable, suffering is optional. Loss is unavoidable, grief isn't. Death is certain. And life, well, life isn't certain. Its uncertainty, unpredictability, even irrationality, make it what it is: worthwhile, a blessing. You can see its attributes as appalling, boring and cunning or as adventurous, beautiful and captivating. Your choice. That's the ABC of life.

As in a game of Scrabble, what letters end up on your rack are not in your hands, but what words you coin and where you place them are a matter of skill and knowledge.

The less ignorant you are in vocabulary, the more chance you have of scoring. The faster you empty your rack, the higher the odds of getting better letters and more options. If you don't let go of the existing letters or crib about how unfortunate you are, you lose your chance of scoring. Life is no different.

The alphabet is the same, it's just what words you construct with the letters available to you that makes all the difference to what you feel about everything. Yes, absolutely everything.

Fill your heart with loving-kindness, your time with noble actions, your mind with good thoughts, and suffering will disappear from your life, like sadness from a content heart. You will realize your soul, your self.

Acchedyo 'yam adāhyo 'yam akledyo 'śoṣya eva ca…

(Bhagavad Gita 2.24)

Needles can't prick your soul nor can fire burn it.
Water can't rot it and heat can't dry it.

And snakes you ask, what about the snakes of attachment? Well, those a yogi wraps around his/her neck and yet remains unharmed.

This is the path of lasting peace.

THE GIFTS OF HURT

Do adversities really have the power to transform us?

A famous Zen monk was at a *Bonenkai* (lit. forget-the-year party) dinner being hosted by a rich nobleman. The who's who of the city mingling with each other lent an intimidating colour to the party for any casual observer. Stunning geishas, a lavish spread comprising premium sake and food, and pleasant fragrances coursing through the hall, all drove the five senses towards sheer indulgence.

An aristocrat approached the Zen monk with deference and said, 'I don't mean to offend you, master, but can I ask you a question?'

The monk raised his hand a little in response, palm facing up.

'They say that you are enlightened, that you have this calming aura and glow,' the man whispered. 'But I could say the same about that geisha.' The aristocrat pointed towards an immaculately dressed woman, donning a silk kimono with floral patterns. Every aspect of hers, from her hairdo to her painted toes, seemed like a work of art. 'In fact, she's far more pleasant to look at. She evokes desire and subdues my pride with her mere form,' the aristocrat added.

'What then,' he continued, 'is the difference between you and her?'

'Fair enough,' the monk replied. 'I'll answer your question at the right moment.'

A few cups of tea later, the same geisha came to the Zen master and bowed before him.

'Ah yes, you!' the master exclaimed. 'I would like to offer you a gift.'

'Anything from you is a blessing,' said the geisha.

From a small hibachi filled with burning coals, the master picked a glowing ember with his chopsticks.

After a moment's hesitation, the geisha, immediately wrapping her kimono sleeves around her hands, extended them and took the hot coal from the master. She then dashed to the kitchen and dropped it in a pan of water. In the process, although her hands remained unhurt, her silk kimono had been ruined. Next, she went into the vanity room, changed into a new robe, fixed her make-up and returned to the party hall.

'Thank you for that,' she said to the master. 'And, I have a return gift for you.'

The master bobbed his head smilingly. The geisha turned to the hibachi, and picking up a burning coal with a pair of tongs, extended it towards him.

'Just the thing I was looking for!' the master said, and whipping out his *kiseru*, i.e., his smoking pipe, he lit it with the coal.

'*Bonenkai*!' he hollered. 'Don't just forget the year, forget the past. Let bygones be bygones.'

The aristocrat, who had been observing what passed between the geisha and the monk, leaned in and said quietly. 'Master! I've got my answer.'

Sometimes, life will offer you a burning coal when you are least prepared. Worse, when you don't even deserve it. Don't burn yourself with that unexpected offering. Instead, use it to strengthen your position, to forge ahead. It is neither a walk in the park nor does it come naturally to us – to not burn oneself with the burning coal – but it can be learned and mastered. I say it's hard work, because a momentary lapse of mindfulness is enough to make us forget all the wisdom in the world and we end up grabbing the cinder, hurting not only ourselves but those on whom we may hurl it.

But let's face it: it's not always easy to be mindful or to maintain our calm. In fact, to maintain an exalted state as that is nearly impossible in our chaotic world, a world where ever-changing circumstances spring up new surprises on us, like an expert illusionist conjuring up objects out of thin air. And that's the thing you see: the wisdom to know that whatever be the cause of your grief, it's temporary, that it's not going to be there forever. So, take it easy, take a deep breath, it's not the end of the world.

Just like our desires and emotions are cyclical, so are the good and bad times in our lives. It is absolutely impossible that each day will turn out the way you expect it to, or that every time only pleasing news will knock on your door. At times, situations are undesirable and unpleasant, but we can't avoid them. We have to deal with them. As they say, someone's got to make the trains run on time. Granted, it's not always feasible to deal with unpleasant situations with a pleasant mood, but it is possible to handle them with patience.

yoga-sthaḥ kuru karmāṇi saṅgaṁ tyaktvā dhanañjaya
siddhy-asiddhyoḥ samo bhūtvā samatvaṁ yoga uchyate.

(Bhagavad Gita 2.48)

'O, the finest archer!' Krishna says to Arjuna, 'the yoga of equanimity is to maintain your steadfastness in the face of both success and failure, it is to act with a degree of detachment.'

I'm often asked, shouldn't we be passionate about our pursuits? Of course, you should be, that's correct. But detachment is not resignation, but the understanding that to make objective decisions, I must, now and again, distance myself from my pursuit so I may gain a different and a better frame of reference. It is only then that you get to see the complete picture, the three sides of the coin: left, right and the edge of the coin.

Detachment is not laziness or avoidance. If anything, it is razor-sharp awareness and a heightened state of consciousness. When parents allow a child to go far away to pursue his/her dreams, they need a certain degree of detachment to put the best interests of their child ahead of their own preferences. Without that dispassion, it would simply not be possible to allow oneself to accept the distance. The good news is that detachment can be learned; you can turn it into a conscious practice by meditating on the impermanent nature of this world as well as the vastness of this universe. Detachment helps you put things in perspective.

One day, a woman noticed her overweight husband sucking in his tummy while weighing himself on the bathroom scale.

'Hehe!' she chuckled. 'That's not gonna help.'

'Sure, it will,' the husband replied. 'It's the only way I can see the numbers.'

Draw in when you need to. Others may not understand why you are doing so, but as long as you know it, that's all that mostly matters.

As Shakespeare wrote in *As You Like It*, 'Sweet are the uses of adversity, which, like the toad, ugly and venomous, wears yet a precious jewel in its head.' The gifts of hurt are something like that. They teach us, elevate us, and above all, force us to connect with our highest state of consciousness for answers and solutions. Painful but useful. Inconvenient but inevitable.

In this conditional world, our attachments blind us and crush us, they don't do us any good. The day you realize and internalize this truth, your life will never be the same again. Don't take the ember or hurl it. Put it to use. Simply be mindful. It helps.

Be aware that transience and impermanence are the ways of the samsara. Let's be compassionate and graceful while we are still here. It's worth it.

WAKE UP

Is time really running out for all of us?

Legend has it that Buddha was once delivering a sermon in Jetavana, and in the end, he said, 'Wake up! Time is running out!'

An hour later, he stepped out with his closest disciples, including the ever-serving Ananda and always inquisitive Shariputra. A large number of people were still hanging about, waiting to catch a glimpse of the enlightened sage. The Buddha stopped near the gates in a quiet corner, so the crowd would dissipate and he could pass through. Just then, a woman spotted him and came running towards him.

'Tathagata,' she said bowing, 'I'm a dancer and I'd been scheduled to perform at the mansion of the richest merchant in the city. It had completely slipped my mind, but you are all-knowing. When you concluded by saying, "Wake up! Time is running out!" it reminded me of my commitment today. I can't thank you enough. I will lay half of whatever I receive today, at your feet.'

The Buddha smiled and blessed her.

They had hardly walked a few steps, when a man approached the Buddha and clasped his feet. The Buddha asked him to get up. 'O Shasta,' the man said, 'I know you never judge anyone, so I must confess my truth to you. For months, I've been eyeing the home of a wealthy man that I intend to break in and steal. Today, I saw him attend your discourse and later tell his family that they were leaving for another town. Your last line, "Wake up! Time is running out!" came as a jolt. I know you've given me the signal and I'm going to succeed in my mission tonight. If I get a good bounty, I'll quit stealing forever.'

'Tathagata only preaches the middle way,' the Buddha said to the man, referring to himself in the third person. 'Tathagata would never encourage anyone to do something that harms the well-being of another person.'

'I just know that your final remarks in the sermon were meant for me,' the man said, and took the Buddha's leave with great deference. But before the Buddha could say anything else, the man took to his heels.

'What a weird man!' Shariputra whispered to Ananda, who only chuckled in return.

'Do not judge,' the Buddha gently reprimanded them both.

Soon, word spread that the awakened sage was taking a stroll with his disciples outside the *vihara*[3] and a crowd began gathering again. The Buddha decided it was better to go back.

Just then an old man, well-dressed and adorned in fineries befitting someone affluent, stopped the Buddha in his tracks. 'O Bhante! Ever merciful Buddha!' he said, with his hands folded and eyes welling up, 'All my life I ran after material things, chasing this goal and that. More fame, more gold, luxurious mansions, debauchery, deceit and immoral thoughts – that's the summary of my life. For whom, for what, I wonder ... Your discourse opened my eyes today. Particularly when you made the closing statement, "Wake up! Time is running out!" with such conviction, I knew instantly it was for me. I have decided to withdraw from material endeavours and work diligently towards nirvana. How will I ever repay you?'

The Buddha blessed the man and returned to his abode where trees, birds, deer, and quiet privacy awaited him.

Ananda washed his feet and Shariputra offered him coconut water. Anuruddha and Subhuti began fanning him, while Nanda and Upali filled buckets of water to sprinkle on the thatched walls of the Buddha's resting cottage to make it cool.

'Pay attention, my spiritual sons,' the Buddha said and called them closer. 'Tathagata made the same statement to the entire congregation, but it meant different things to different people. Each one interpreted it according to their understanding, convenience and circumstances. Hence, I say, your liberation depends on you alone.'

Have you noticed that we are in conflict with another when the other person doesn't approve of our actions or we, theirs? When their actions don't feel right or, more importantly, their perspective is not the same as ours? They may have grown up in the same culture, they may even have studied in the same school as yours, heck, they may even have grown up in the same household as you did, and yet that does not mean they see the world through the same set of eyes.

The Buddha placed great emphasis on 'right view', i.e., a view that is non-violent (in thought, speech and action). That, I am responsible for what I feel, and above all, whatever I experience is the result of either my actions or my conditioning (read perspective of life). Indeed, the noble Eightfold Path begins with a right view, because, according to him, and I concur, all else falls apart in the absence of a wholesome understanding. Simply put, 'right view' comprises the following:

1. Our actions have consequences.
2. Death is not the end.
3. Our actions and beliefs have consequences after death.

If two people could see the world the same way, they would have no conflict with each other. And usually, that's where the whole struggle lies: helping the other person see your perspective or you seeing theirs.

~

Pulitzer Prize-winning American writer Upton Sinclair once said, 'It is difficult to get a man to understand something when his salary depends on not understanding it!'

I have realized that this 'salary' is not always monetary in nature. It often comprises nothing more than our tightly held beliefs in the form of the skewed morality and social conditioning we experience at personal, interpersonal and professional levels, at all times.

Achieving the desired outcome in any situation depends almost entirely on your getting the other person to buy your story. Peace between two people or entities can only exist if they can see each other's perspective. Think about it. This is the root cause of all conflict, the basis of our struggles across the board: the other person or party neither understands nor can seem to accept why we do what we do. And vice versa too: we can neither accept nor understand their ways.

It takes patience, empathy and wisdom (even guidance, at times) to shift the paradigm, to drop the coloured lens, and to have the courage to see the world as is. You can't see what lies at the surface of a pond unless you stop stirring the water. To quiet the mind when it's raging with judgements and analysis, so you can see things as they are, is what meditation is about. It is what *I* mean by 'right view'.

~

'How come you are always happy?' Mulla Nasruddin's friend asked him one day.

'It's very simple, my friend,' said Mulla. 'I have a beautiful and intelligent wife. No matter how stressful my day is, I go home and spend a quiet, intimate evening with her and all my stress is gone.'

'Really?'

'It works, trust me!'

His friend thanked him for the wise counsel. Some two weeks later, while Mulla was eating his dinner, he heard a knock on the door. It was his friend, looking rather down.

'You, here? Now? All okay?' Mulla exclaimed.

'I'm very stressed, Mulla,' he said, 'and I'm ready to spend a quiet evening with your wife.'

Now then, you know what I *don't* mean by seeing the world from another person's perspective. It is not that we must do what they do in their world. Often, it simply means that we bring a whole range of possibilities to our world, so that we don't become stagnant and regressive. After all, progress at any level is nothing more than the acceptance of a new way of life, a new dimension, another perspective. Challenge yourself.

The journey to a new life begins with a new way of thinking. Wake up! Time is running out…

LEAVE YOUR REGRETS BEHIND

In the ceaseless movement of the wheel of time, is it possible to leave our regretful past behind?

There was once a lady, a social activist, who helped people get off alcohol. It was a small town and every time she heard that someone had taken to or was drinking, she would immediately go to them wherever they were with a small group of people, advising them on the ill-effects of alcohol. The number of drinkers in that community actually went down, but that was because no one wanted to face her.

One day, a visitor from a distant town was sitting in the only remaining bar in the town and enjoying his drink. As soon as the activist found out, she rushed to the spot with some others.

'Sir,' she said enthusiastically, 'you do know that alcohol is not the solution to your problems.'

'Tell me about it,' he replied with equal zeal, 'but hey, it does help me forget my problems for a little while.'

The lady saw the futility of her argument, and adopting a different line, said, 'It has terrible effects on your health and can even hasten your demise.'

'I'm not afraid of death. For all I know, I could have an accident and be dead the moment I step out of this place. I may as well live now.'

'Fine,' she sighed. 'How long have you been drinking?'

'Every day for the last twenty years. And I've no health issues.'

'How much do you spend every time you drink?'

'$10.'

'So that's $10 x 365 = $3650 every year?'

'Sounds right.'

'And over twenty years, it would be a whopping sum of $3650 x 20 = $73,000.'

'Wow, I never thought like that!' the man said, this time putting his drink down.

'Exactly! And if we factor in the interest earned, you're looking at $1,00,000!' the activist said animatedly. 'And, with $1,00,000, mister, you could have bought a BMW 7-series!'

'Your logic is impeccable, lady! Now, may I ask you a question?'

The woman nodded triumphantly and looked at the others in the group who were amply impressed with her intelligent reasoning.

'Do you drink?' he asked politely.

'Of course not! I have not touched alcohol in the last thirty years!'

'Far out, eh,' the man exclaimed. 'So, what colour is your BMW?'

'Excuse me?' she said, a little puzzled.

'I mean if you didn't drink, you must have saved $10 every day and bought a BMW, I suppose.'

At this, the lady stomped her foot and stormed out of the bar.

I am not, by any means, including this joke in the book to endorse the consumption of alcohol in any way. I do have an important point to make though.

We all have regrets in life. I'm not even talking about grave regrets of wrongdoing or transgressions. I'm talking about the simple noise in the head. That chattering of the mind that tells us how our life could have been, would have been or should have been, had we done this, that or the other. Like the activist, the blabbering mind shows up just when you sit down to relax or do something that you enjoy. It nudges you, nags you and reminds you about your choices in the past. Choices you were once proud of, but not any more. You start to feel low, a feeling of regret rains down on you, washing aside your peace. The present looks dull, the future bleak. You wish you'd lived differently.

In this moment of weakness, when you are laden with regret, the mind begins to focus on what you could have done in the past to have a glorious present. And as they say, in hindsight vision is 20/20. The truth is, endless analysis of your past is mostly blabbering of the restless mind. For, chances are, you did what you thought was best at the time. And, that, in my view, is good enough.

What matters infinitely more is focusing on your present and making it worthwhile, for the present of today will be the past of tomorrow.

Before leaps and running, comes walking and crawling. It's never too late to make a commitment to your future. Don't count the weeks, months or years. Simply keep walking one step at a time. And remember, if you don't embark on your journey now, you will only lose more time. For, time is passing anyway.

If you want to get a sense of time, then simply look at a stopwatch (your phone will have one) where you can see milliseconds zipping away. That's how fast life is going by. Millions of creatures are born and millions die in a fraction of these blindingly fast moments. The wheel of time churns relentlessly. Moments gone will *never* come back. So, act wisely and mindfully in the living present. The past is dead, it has nothing new for you. And the future is just the present of tomorrow. Now is the only living moment, the only true moment in which life actually exists in its entirety.

~

A rich man walks to his Bentley in the parking lot and finds the headlights broken with a fair bit of damage to the bumper. Exasperated, he vainly looks around to see if the offender is in sight. He is, however, relieved to see that there's a slip tucked under the windshield wiper. It reads: 'Sorry. I just backed into your Bentley. Some people around are nodding and smiling at me because they think I'm leaving my name and other details. But I'm not.'

And so it is with life. For no direct fault of our own, it seems, sometimes our present turns out to be different than what we envisaged it to be all along, and we think life will give us some indication of how to go about fixing it. But there's none.

One way to get past your past and your regrets is to give your life meaning. Once you discover the meaning, the purpose of your life, you no longer remain the old you. The new you is born in the same body. It becomes a whole lot easier to shed your old tendencies as your newfound meaning becomes your guiding and driving force.

LIFE IS A STRUGGLE

Is life really a big struggle or is it a matter of perspective?

I go through anywhere between two to three thousand emails every month. Ninety per cent of these emails are from people who are struggling with one thing or the other. Some of them are tired of battling and resisting, they are at a crossroads, they don't know what to do, they say. In many cases, they write, 'Life's been too hard on me.' Life is a struggle and it's been like that for them ever since, they say.

Yes, life can be hard, life can be a struggle. But then again, is it really any different for anybody else? Those who lack money think that people with money have it easy. Those with wealth and stressful businesses think others with simple nine-to-five jobs have it easier. The healthy think the wealthy are better, the wealthy think happy people are better. Yet, there are many who are healthy, wealthy and everything else you can imagine, and they are still depressed, they still struggle to go through their lives. The truth is that that's what life is about. For everyone.

As long as we are working towards accomplishing anything, there are going to be obstacles. Some see these obstacles as challenges and others see them as struggle. People may change, things may be different, situations may be more favourable, circumstances more pleasant, but that doesn't mean challenges will cease to be. There will always be hurdles. Besides, I've realized that when people talk about struggle, they are mostly referring to challenges. And, whether we see a problem as an opportunity or a barrier, it's a matter of perspective, it's a question of mindset, it's a personal choice. Here's an interesting story for you:

On a tree in his backyard, a man saw a cocoon of a butterfly. He observed it every day for the next few days. One day, he saw a tiny opening in the cocoon with a bright caterpillar inside. It was at a larval stage. He observed the grub for hours and saw it grapple to come out of the swathe. Every day, he witnessed it struggling, but with each passing day it was out a bit more, wings were forming on its body. The cocoon was becoming more taut and cramped for the growing larva.

Seeing it struggling to free itself of the flexed cocoon, the man decided to help the butterfly. He snipped off the cocoon and out came the butterfly effortlessly. It fell straight to the ground though, its body swollen and its wings shrivelled. The man sat there, expectantly, waiting to see the butterfly take off, but it never did. It crawled around helplessly with its bulbous body. Its wings never grew fully and it couldn't fly. Before long, it perished. What the man saw as struggle, was Nature's way of preparing the butterfly for survival.

Our struggles shape us, they define us. I'm not saying all struggle is good, but I'm asking if it's really struggle. How does a bodybuilder build his body? He has to undergo resistance training if he's serious about growing and chiseling his muscles. He can look upon lifting weights as a struggle or a rewarding task. His state of mind will depend on his perspective. And, more importantly, the results, in turn, will depend on his mindset.

Our Nature has evolved with challenges. It will continue to stretch you based on your capabilities. You cannot reduce the magnitude of those challenges. If you have something to offer, Nature will extract it from you. We are not the centre of the Universe, but a tiny artifact in Nature's grand scheme. But yes, you can reduce the intensity, frequency and number of those challenges. How? Simplify your life. Start by decluttering. Once you start to simplify everything about you, never again will you look upon adversity as struggle. I'm not saying you'll consider every challenge as an opportunity either. But you won't be deterred by it.

Life may be a straight road, but it is rarely a smooth one. Certain stretches, some aspects of it may be velvety, but overall, it is topsy-turvy to keep you alive, to keep you awake. Enjoy the ride. Imagine you are standing on the roadside and moments of life are passing by like the traffic on a freeway. Life doesn't stop for anyone, it doesn't stop to listen to complaints or compliments. Our earth, even other planets, don't stop rotating or revolving, not even for a moment, lest they lose their existence.

The intricate, interdependent and fascinating play of Nature never comes to a halt. Life can't afford to stop. If you want to enjoy it, you'll have to learn to negotiate with it.

This life is real and transient, like the bubbles in froth. Love it, live it before it pops.

SAMSARA

What is the ultimate truth?

The other day I read the story of Patacara in Anna Prajna Douglas's *The Hidden Lamp: Stories of Twenty-five Centuries of Awakened Women.*[4] As follows (partially paraphrased):

Some 2500 years ago, Patacara was born into a rich family in India, but eventually ran off to marry a pageboy. A tragedy hit her life, when Patacara was about to deliver her second child. She lost her entire family in a single day. Legend has it that her husband was bitten by a poisonous snake the same day her newborn baby was carried off by a hawk. Within a span of minutes, her parents' house collapsed, killing her brother, mother and father, while her older son drowned in a river.

Mad with grief, Patacara tore off her clothes and wandered around like a lunatic. Naked and unkempt, she roamed about aimlessly for a long time, until she meandered into Jetavana where the Buddha was teaching.

Seeing her despicable and undignified state, some of the senior monks got up to drive her out of the sage's sight. The Buddha raised his hand to stop them.

Patacara fell at his feet. Her tears had long dried. Her hair was knotted, her body stinking and soiled. Unaware of her appearance, she alternated between howling and sobbing.

'O noble lady,' the Buddha spoke softly, 'be mindful.'

At his compassionate words, Patacara experienced a sense of normalcy and instantly realized that she was stark naked. A man offered his cloak and she covered herself. She narrated the tragedy and begged the Buddha to help her.

'I can't help you,' the Buddha said. 'No one can. For countless lives you have wept for loved ones. Your tears could fill the four oceans. But no one can be in a secure, hiding place from suffering. Knowing this, a wise person walks the path of awakening.'

Patacara's whole being was overwhelmed with a deep sense of peace at the Buddha's words and in his presence. The sage then spoke the following verses from the *Dhammapada* (288–89): 'There are no sons to give shelter, no father, no family for one seized by Death, no shelter among kin. Conscious of this, the wise, restrained by virtue, should clear the path that goes to Nirvana.'

Patacara was ordained in his sangha and the Buddha instructed her to meditate on impermanence.

'Patacara,' he said, 'everyone dies one day. All human beings must die. It is better to see the truth of impermanence even for just a moment than to live for a hundred years and not know it.'

~

Impermanence is the essence of existence. Our world, this universe is surviving and intact because it's constantly changing. And at the root of our struggles is the quest for permanence, to somehow vainly ensure that any good in our lives must remain as is. Harmony and evolution, however, flourish on a different principle – the principle of freedom.

You kill whatever you cling to. For anything to survive, it must have a degree of freedom. Imagine if the skies held on to clouds, never letting them go. There would have been no rains, the oceans would have eventually dried up, and the planet would have ceased to exist. Nature sustains on the principle of impermanence. Awakening is to be at ease with your ever-changing life. It may not be easy, but it's entirely doable.

If someone doesn't want to be in your life, let that person go. There's no wisdom in holding on to a partner, person, employer or a thing. Everything and everyone must ultimately perish. Separation from all that we love is not a question of 'if' but 'when'. It's inevitable, only a matter of time. Our childhood, adolescence, youth, old age, all phases pass. Those who loved you deeply yesterday may loathe you tomorrow. The memories of the one who you loved deeply once, may only give you grief now. This is samsara – cyclical and transient.

The moment it dawns on you that nothing lasts forever and you feel okay with it, enlightenment is imminent.

It is always followed by a state of perfect tranquility and harmony.

At the breakfast table, a woman said to her husband, 'Honey, last night, I dreamed that you gave me a necklace of pearls. What do you think it means?'

Smiling, the man kissed his wife and whispered, 'You'll know tonight.'

Surely enough, that evening, he came home with a small, beautifully wrapped package. With a playful grin, he gave it to his wife. She jumped with joy before settling onto the couch to open her gift. She undid the tape, and unwrapped the package to see a book that was titled *The Meaning of Dreams*.

We dream of life giving us a necklace of pearls when it's actually planning to give us the meaning of our dream. This mismatch is the chief cause behind why most people are forever riding an emotional roller-coaster. They want permanence, some guarantee, when there's none. The truth is: absolutely everything is transient; a passing phase.

> *samaya pāe phala hota hai samaya pāe jharī jāta,*
> *sadā rahe nahīṃ eka sī, kā Rahīma pachtaat.*

> When the time comes, trees are laden with leaves and fruits, and then, with time, it sheds them. What are you brooding over, says Rahim, when all phases of life pass eventually.

This is one of the most potent self-affirmations to imbibe the truth of impermanence in your heart. Whenever you are down or disturbed, whenever you feel lost or low, just touch your heart and tell yourself that this time will pass. That suffering, too, is a part of life. It's one of the seasons. Knock on your heart with a gentle hand and say that this trying phase won't stay forever.

Whenever you are over the moon or think you have the best life, tap your heart again and remind yourself that this time won't last either. This, too, is one of the fleeting seasons. It has a strange but positive effect on your peace of mind. You feel more centred and grounded.

In the fullness of time, the present moment must make way for the next present moment. The present must yield to the future. This ceaseless play of moments emerging and passing is what gives beauty to the unpredictability of our lives. It's beyond comprehension or control. At best, you can live it, love it and rejoice in it. With gratitude. This is the path of peace. And peace, I may add, is the only real treasure. The rest are temporary acquisitions.

IMPERMANENCE

Is nothing perceivable? Permanent? Are clouds, the moon, the stars, our planet, and everything in it, constantly changing?

Sometimes, I wonder why we are so averse to adversities. We label everything that doesn't fall in line with our expectations from life, as suffering. Whether that be a difficult person, situation or problem, whatever rattles us becomes undesirable to us. Very quickly. We want it discarded. I don't think the issue is with expectations per se, for our desires are at the root of our progress – material or spiritual. The real problem is with the unrealistic nature of our expectations, the greatest being our desire that anything good in our life should stay as it is.

Padmasambhava, commonly known as Guru Rinpoche, was a young eighth-century Indian mystic who spent most of his adulthood in Tibet. His charm and enigma was such that he was revered and loved by everyone who ever met him, even briefly, except there were some, among the royalty, and a few commoners, who envied him. People lavishly showered on Rinpoche affection, praise and gifts. The king offered him a permanent place in his own palace and treated him like a son. He seemed destined for the affluence and power he enjoyed. He was a bold speaker, who spoke his truth without fear. They even predicted that one day, Rinpoche would be the Sovereign of Tibet.

Legend has it, that once, while dancing in ecstasy, holding the king's ritual implements consisting of a bell and a trident, Rinpoche hurled them in the air from his rooftop. They fell on to the street below, the trident landing on the head of a passer-by, killing him on the spot. Those jealous of Rinpoche seized the opportunity and a propaganda was launched. It worked, too, and soon the public was outraged. His youth was termed inexperience, his truth arrogance. The locals pushed for the sentence that Rinpoche be banished from the community.

Charming Rinpoche, who was once predicted to be Tibet's Sovereign, spent the rest of his life in wilderness. That one incident, however, was enough to awaken Rinpoche, to bring him face-to-face with the reality of this world – impermanence.

Sometimes, that's all you need, just one incident to awaken you. Just one wake-up call to help you see what this samsara truly is – irrational and impermanent. Such a life-transforming incident then changes your perspective forever. Your old tendencies continue to surface and haunt you, but the awakened you, handles life differently.

This world can offer you anything you fancy except permanence. Those who love you today, will grow out one day. No matter how stable and permanent anything may appear, it is going to wither away. Nothing here is designed to last. Forests burn, mountains move, rivers dry up, oceans retreat, glaciers melt, people die. However gigantic or miniscule, such as heat in fire or oil in olives, the inherent nature of all things perceivable is impermanent.

If we could be mindful about the transient nature of this world, adversities won't hurt as much. When you take it as a given that those in your favour today may be against you tomorrow or vice-versa, their behaviour won't surprise you any more. When you are very happy, just remind yourself that it's not going to last. And when you are very sad, ask yourself why. Not why this is happening to me, but why I am sad. What's bothering me? Why am I reacting like this? Does this befit me? Is it wise? And so on. A cool breeze of mindfulness will soothe your parched existence almost immediately.

Both happiness and sadness, like pleasure and pain, are fleeting feelings. It's just that we so despise sadness and pain that the moment there's even the slightest trace of it in our lives, we are taken aback. One fruit fly landing in your salad is enough to ruin the whole experience of a great meal.

Suffering or sadness is not wrong or right. It just is. If you want to have any chance at going with the flow of life (and enjoying the process), it's imperative to remind yourself that nothing is permanent, that suffering is okay. I'm not talking about mass suffering, such as children dying of hunger. That can never be okay. The strong should protect the weak. I'm referring to individual suffering. The type that makes us feel that life is worthless.

At the root of such suffering is the clinging to our expectations from life, as if we really know how life ought to be. We forget that everyone and everything will be separated from us one day. No one here truly belongs to us permanently. Each one of us is battling with his or her own issues. It sounds grim but truth is generally like that.

In his beautiful poem, 'The Patriot', Robert Browning captures the essence of this transient world. The same person who was given a royal welcome a year ago is now abandoned by his people. He is misunderstood and being sentenced for something he didn't do. But he takes heart believing that at least God knows, and that even if he is executed now, it won't matter because he will rest in heaven.

It was roses, roses, all the way,
With myrtle mixed in my path like mad:
The house-roofs seemed to heave and sway,
The church-spires flamed, such flags they had,
A year ago on this very day.

The air broke into a mist with bells,
The old walls rocked with the crowd and cries.
Had I said, 'Good folk, mere noise repels –
But give me your sun from yonder skies!'
They had answered, 'And afterward, what else?'

Alack, it was I who leaped at the sun
To give it my loving friends to keep!
Nought man could do have I left undone:
And you see my harvest, what I reap
This very day, now a year is run.

There's nobody on the house-tops now –
Just a palsied few at the windows set;
For the best of the sight is, all allow,
At the Shambles' Gate – or, better yet,
By the very scaffold's foot, I trow.

I go in the rain, and, more than needs,
A rope cuts both my wrists behind;
And I think, by the feel, my forehead bleeds,
For they fling, whoever has a mind,
Stones at me for my year's misdeeds.

Thus I entered, and thus I go!
In triumphs, people have dropped down dead.
'Paid by the world, what dost thou owe
Me?' – God might question; now instead,
'Tis God shall repay: I am safer so.

That is not to say that people don't love each other, or that this is a false world. It's just that it's all temporary and transient. There are absolutely no guarantees. Reminding yourself of it will help you walk the path of dharma. It will give you the strength to make the right choices and speak the right words. And the more righteous your life, your conduct, the greater peace you experience at heart. It's that simple, really.

⁓

Mulla Nasruddin was visiting a town for two weeks. Having some free time on his hands, he went for a day's indulgence at a Turkish hamam. Seeing him so plainly dressed, the workers quickly concluded that this customer could do without any service. They gave him a small bar of soap, an old towel and hardly paid him any attention. Mulla was pretty much on his own. The most inexperienced masseur gave him a lousy massage and scrub. Instead of complaining though, Mulla gave the masseur a generous tip of fifty dinars on his way out and thanked the workers at the hamam profusely. The staff was shocked at this hefty gratuity.

A week later, Mulla visited the hamam again. The staff now knew what a rich and generous man he was. They gave him the most exclusive treatment in the form of royal greetings, fluffy towels, a gentle and invigorating scrub, and a long massage. A copious amount of pleasantly hot water was poured on Mulla. He was served Arabian tea with dates. Who knew what all he might include in the tip when happy and satisfied, they thought. In the end though, Mulla frowned at them and handed a tip of a just one dinar.

'Excuse me, sir,' the worker couldn't resist asking, 'last time, we barely served you and yet you tipped us fifty dinars. This time, we gave you the finest we could and you give us only one dinar. We don't understand. We are at our wit's end.'

'Oh, that,' Mulla said casually, while walking out, 'the last tip was for this week's service. And today's tip is for last week's visit.'

So, it is with our world, too. How you are served and loved depends a great deal on how you are perceived and what all you can do for others. Love demands sacrifice. It's neither good nor bad. It's simply the way our mind works. And, it's not only the others. We, too, love and serve others based on our own criteria. Ultimately, everything is cyclical, conditional and transient.

Your happiness is completely in your hands, as is your awakening. The more mindful you are with your words, actions and intentions, the less aggression you harbour towards others and yourself. The gentler you are with yourself, the happier you will be. More happiness equals goodness. Our world could do with some more.

Be kind. At all times. And you will be awakened. Samsara, even if transient and illusory, couldn't be more beautiful then.

II
LONELINESS

THE CENTRE OF YOUR LIFE

Will loving someone selflessly make us complete?

There's a beautiful story in Srimad Bhagavatam.

Impressed by his knowledge, King Yadu enquired an *avadhuta,* an enlightened master, about his guru, who answered that he had had many gurus, including a prostitute.

'A prostitute?' the king scorned.

'Yes, why not?' said the *avadhuta*. 'Hear what I learned from her.' And he went on to narrate the story of Pingala.

Pingala was a glamorous courtesan in the ancient city of Videha. With her red lips, like freshly cut strawberries, beautiful, buxom and seductive, she smelled of exotic flowers. Just the sight of her was enough to evoke desire. Indeed, her stunning beauty was the reason why she was made courtesan in the first place, for the kings and powerful merchants would otherwise break into fights over her. Pingala enjoyed royal patronage unlike any other courtesan in the country.

Through the years, she had learned to practise the craft of love with the same detachment as a doctor's towards his or her patient. And yet, as is the way of love – mysterious and unreasonable, she lost her heart to a prince. The young prince promised to visit her on a certain date.

Pingala turned away all other patrons upon one excuse or another that day. She took a long beauty bath, had herself anointed with various unguents and herbal packs. She had her hair plaid carefully with mogra, jasmine and other flower buds. She donned her crimson red saree made from the finest silk. Her forehead, ears, neck, wrists, ankles were adorned with expensive ornaments of gold, rubies, emeralds and diamonds. One could have easily mistaken her for an empress.

All decked up and ready, she eagerly waited for her prince, to be in his loving embrace and see him from up close. Afternoon was fading away into dusk, but the prince never showed up. Meanwhile, many men who came to seek her favours were turned away. There was only one person she wanted to see. Feelings of loyalty and love washed away all other desires from her heart; she wanted to belong only to the prince.

Every few minutes, her anklets would tinkle, her fineries would chime, as she'd run to the gates to find out if the prince had arrived, if, accidentally, the guards might have barred his entry. She would chastise them to be more watchful. She would peep through, with great anticipation, to see every palanquin and every chariot that passed. Maybe this was the prince, she'd think. Even her handmaids were surprised to see their mistress so anxious. To keep her mouth fresh and red, Pingala didn't eat the whole day; she only chewed betel leaves.

Twilight turned to darkness; the night thickened. Pingala lost her appetite, and yet she was growing more desperate by the moment. Stars appeared, twinkling here and there in the sky. A few more hours passed, and the full moon appeared, along with some more stars. The crickets clittered, and the chakora bird sang every now and then, making a long mating call. The wait and love in Pingala's heart were alive as ever, but there was no sign of the prince.

She spent the whole night awake. Her eyes grew tired, and countless times Pingala adjusted her dress and embellishments. Tens of times she saw herself in the mirror and redid her make-up. Several times, she sprinkled fragrance on herself. All to remain perfect for when the prince arrived. But he never did. The flower buds in her hair were wilting away, a brownish tinge gradually grasping the fair jasmine flowers.

Just before the breaking of dawn, while people were waking from a night's sleep, Pingala, too, woke up from her ignorance with a deep realization. The *avadhuta* told the king:

na hy aṅgājāta-nirvedo
deha-bandhaṁ jihāsati
yathā vijñāna-rahito
manujo mamatāṁ nṛpa

(Srimad Bhagavatam, 11.8.29)

O King, just as a human being bereft of spiritual knowledge never desires to give up his false sense of proprietorship over many material things, similarly, a person who has not developed detachment never desires to give up the bondage of the material body.

Pingala, however, rose above her false sense of existence that day. She experienced great *vairagya,* detachment, and *ananda,* bliss. She realized that she was already complete and didn't need another man to fulfil her. That the one she should have loved, the one for whom she wouldn't have to wait day and night, the one who would never abandon her, was already inside her – God.

Pingala's narrative continues in Srimad Bhagavatam as follows:

Piṅgalovāca
aho me moha-vitatiṁ
paśyatāvijitātmanaḥ
yā kāntād asataḥ kāmaṁ
kāmaye yena bāliśā ||30||

santaṁ samīpe ramaṇaṁ rati-pradaṁ
vitta-pradaṁ nityam imaṁ vihāya
akāma-daṁ duḥkha-bhayādhi-śoka-
moha-pradaṁ tuccham ahaṁ bhaje 'jñā ||31||

aho mayātmā paritāpito vṛthā
sāṅketya-vṛttyāti-vigarhya-vārtayā

strainān narād yārtha-tṛṣo 'nuśocyāt
krītena vittaṁ ratim ātmanecchatī ||32||

yad asthibhir nirmita-vaṁśa-vaṁsya-sthūṇaṁ
tvacā roma-nakhaiḥ pinaddham
kṣaran-nava-dvāram agāram etad
viṇ-mūtra-pūrṇaṁ mad upaiti kānyā ||33||

videhānāṁ pure hy asminn
aham ekaiva mūḍha-dhīḥ
yānyam icchanty asaty asmād
ātma-dāt kāmam acyutāt ||34||

Pingala said: Just see how greatly illusioned I am! Because I cannot control my mind, just like a fool I desire lusty pleasure from an insignificant man. ||30||

I am so ignorant that I have given up the service of that person who, being eternally situated within my heart, is actually most dear to me. That most dear one is the Lord of the universe, who is the bestower of real love and happiness and the source of all prosperity. Although He is in my own heart, I have completely neglected Him. Instead I have ignorantly served insignificant men who can never satisfy my real desires and who have simply brought me unhappiness, fear, anxiety, lamentation and illusion. ||31||

Oh, how I have uselessly tortured my own soul! I have sold my body to lusty, greedy men who are

> themselves objects of pity. How ignorant of me that I hoped to get money and sexual pleasure from my profession. ||32||
>
> This material body is like a house in which I, the soul, am living. The bones forming my spine, ribs, arms and legs are like the beams, crossbeams and pillars of the house, and the whole structure, which is full of stool and urine, is covered by skin, hair and nails. The nine doors leading into this body are constantly excreting foul substances. Besides me, what woman could be so foolish as to devote herself to this material body, thinking that she might find pleasure and love in this contraption? ||33||
>
> Certainly in this city of Videha I alone am completely foolish. I neglected the Supreme Personality of Godhead, who awards us everything, even our original spiritual form, and instead I desired to enjoy sense gratification with many men. ||34||
>
> (Srimad Bhagavatam[5], Srila Prabhupada Translation, 11.08.30–34)

I'm not sure if I've much more to add or say; Pingala's story is a message in itself.

Somewhere, it's not just her story but every person's who has ever loved anyone and sought to be loved back in return. After meeting thousands of people, I've observed that the most common cause of grief is not people's expectations from their relationships but generally the relationship itself. All worldly relationships are bound to have challenges, predominantly because we want the other person to fulfil us (and the other wants the same from you). Having said that, I'm not suggesting that relationships are bad or that you shouldn't be in one. A great deal of our happiness depends on the quality of our personal and social interactions, after all. The truth still remains that if we don't know how to keep ourselves happy, no one else will ever be able to do that for us.

There's only so much the other person can give you. Ultimately, your happiness depends on your selfless karma as well as on how you treat yourself. Doing something for the one you love is not always selfless. If rather than buying a watch for yourself, you buy a bracelet for your wife, it's certainly thoughtful and caring, but not necessarily selfless, if you see what I mean. You have great emotional investment in such a relationship. Quintessential selflessness is when you do a karma with little or no expectation in return, maybe when you do it with no emotional or any other vested interest of your own. At any rate, my fulfilment in life is my personal responsibility. Who has ever discovered an ocean of happiness by looking up to another person? We must have the courage and wisdom to walk the path of dharma with contentment and gratitude instead of constantly counting on others to fill our cup.

If Pingala's happiness depended on the arrival of her prince and how well he treated, accepted and loved her, she was never going to find permanent happiness, for longing in love and the intensity of feelings are transient.

Besides, it's not possible to love someone without first being fulfilled ourselves. And the feeling of fulfilment is an inner experience. Others can give us a glimpse of it, but in the end, it's your own depth of character and existence that dictates how content you are.

Whatever you seek from others, learn to give it to yourself first. To be selfless in love is to love the other person the way he or she wants to be loved. Start with yourself. Take responsibility. You won't find yourself waiting for someone to knock on your heart's door. Instead, you'll discover that your heart is as big as the sky, it has no doors, it's vast and has ample room for everyone.

And, one last word: you always draw your energy and inspiration from whoever is the centre of your life. In love, you become the one you love. If it's a materialistic person, you'll find yourself becoming increasingly materialistic too. If he or she is a spiritual person, you'll evolve into a calmer person. If he or she is the restless or narcissistic type, you'll feel restless and anxious yourself. If the centre of your life is beauty, divinity, compassion, God and such like, you'll become an embodiment of that. Choose carefully.

A SPIRITUAL ATTITUDE

What is the meaning of having a spiritual attitude towards life?

Subhuti was one of the chief disciples of the Buddha and he had been long wanting to propagate the teachings of his master. One morning, during Buddha's sojourn in Jetavana, just outside his abode Gandhakutir, he prostrated before the Buddha and sought his permission to spread his message far and wide.

'Get up, Subhuti,' said Buddha. 'It's not easy being a teacher. Even if you are speaking beautiful words, there will be plenty who will criticize and condemn you.'

'With your blessings and grace, O Shasta, I'm sure it won't affect me. Do I have Tathagata's permission?'

The Buddha's silence stretched beyond a few minutes; he made no further remarks, while Subhuti remained seated there with his head bowed. Meanwhile, other monks approached the Buddha with urgent tasks relating to Jetavana and other *viharas*, retreat centres, and monasteries that were mushrooming in different parts of

India. Three hours later, the Buddha had his meal and went inside his cottage for his daily rest.

A few more hours passed and when he emerged again for the evening discourse, Subhuti was still outside, his head bowed.

'Subhuti,' Buddha said, 'you are still here. I thought you had your answer from my silence.'

'I'm not wise enough to know the meaning of Tathagata's silence, Lord. No one is.'

The Buddha smiled and assumed his lotus posture.

'What if you go to a village to teach, Subhuti, and people choose not to listen to you? What will you do?'

'I'll not mind, Lord, for I'll remind myself that at least they are not calling me names or accusing me.'

'What if they do that?'

'I'll still smile, O Tathagata, for I'll remind myself that this is a small price to pay for spreading your message. That, they may be doing much worse by abusing me physically.'

'And what if they do that and hurl stones at you?'

'I'll still be all right with Tathagata's grace. I'll remind myself that at least they have not pinned me down and stabbed me?'

'What if they do that?'

'I'll take heart thinking that they have not killed me.'

'And what if, Subhuti,' the Buddha asked, in his usual detached manner, 'they do kill you.'

'I'll be most happy, Tathagata,' Subhuti replied, raising his head for the first time.

Beholding the beautiful form of Buddha, with tearful eyes, he continued, 'For me, nirvana can be attained either dying at Tathagata's feet or by dying spreading Tathagata's message.'

'Subhuti,' the Buddha said, rising from his seat and embracing his disciple, 'you are fit to be a teacher. Morning was merely your test of patience. You have the spiritual attitude required to take on a great cause.'

In this wisdom of a lifetime, nothing else perhaps could spell any clearer the three core virtues that define a person's spiritual attitude. Patience, selflessness and determination. In Subhuti's character, I also see a sense of gratitude and surrender. We can't develop an unconditional spiritual attitude without cultivating patience and selflessness.

Non-fulfilment of desires and expectations is often at the root of human suffering. Why don't people value me? Why doesn't my partner love me? Why isn't the world waiting for me? Why isn't my work appreciated? And so on.

If I start giving a sermon on how expectations are bad, that won't work because you already know all that. We are so compelled and controlled by our emotions and desires that when in their throes, our viewpoint seems so correct and legitimate, no logic works at that time. That, however, can't be the excuse for not evolving spiritually.

And that leads me to the crux of the matter today: a spiritual attitude. Unless we foster a spiritual outlook towards our own life and those of others, we can't really hope to rise above our petty thoughts and emotions. We place too much emphasis on self-comfort, on why I'm being treated or not being treated in a certain way. How about why shouldn't I be more selfless? Why shouldn't I be more giving? Rather than being in the crowd opposing Subhuti, why couldn't I *be* Subhuti?

A spiritual attitude basically means that we don't always put ourselves at the centre of our decisions and actions. Maybe we don't always have to look for what's-in-it-for-me. Why must every generous action of ours be reciprocated? After all, if it's truly selfless, then let it be just that – selfless.

Have you noticed how sometimes we give a gift to someone and want to know what exactly that person did with that gift? And we may even feel hurt if we find out that he or she didn't use it, and passed it on to someone else. That means, we never actually parted with our gift to begin with. Where's the act of giving in that?

If you wish to take on a cause to help others – some cause that makes your existence more useful, which in turn will make your life more fulfilling – developing a spiritual attitude towards life and our world is a must. This essentially means that just because the other person is hurting me, or people disagree with me and don't reciprocate, etc., we will abandon patience, selflessness and compassion. These reasons aren't good enough. And sometimes, the only way of transcending your small personal issues is to devote your energy to bigger ones. To worry or be careworn is our *mula pravriti*, i.e., inherent tendency. We may as well then worry about greater and altruistic causes than be bogged down by our own piddly issues.

Mulla Nasruddin was taking a stroll with his friend when, suddenly, out of nowhere, clouds began to gather in the sky. Before they knew it, it was raining buckets.

'Mulla!' his friend shouted, 'Open your umbrella! Thank God we have one!'

'This umbrella is no good,' Mulla strained to speak under the onslaught of heavy rain. 'It is full of holes.'

'Why on earth are you carrying it around then?'

'How would I know it was going to rain!'

Like Mulla, we carry around our baggage, our me-first umbrella, thinking it will help us, insulate us, but it's full of holes. It can't protect us or those around us. Neither from sunshine nor rain. No doubt, you have to take care of yourself, enjoy yourself and so on, but to go through an entire lifetime doing just that is plain ignorance. It's certainly not spiritual and it definitely won't be fulfilling.

If it's fulfilment you seek, look past yourself. Even past all methods of meditation, yoga and so on. Methods don't necessarily lead to fulfilment. While they may help us become more mindful of our words and actions, at the end of the day, it is our attitude that fuels our fulfilment. The pages of history are replete with selfless saints across all religions, who never did this *kriya* or that, they didn't sit down and practise yoga or meditation as per the yogic scriptures. Were they any less enlightened? I don't think so. What they did possess was a gentle and compassionate world-view.

The more spiritual your perspective, the grander your life becomes. Forgiveness, selflessness, patience, compassion and gratitude naturally flow unrestrained like Himalayan waterfalls during monsoons.

Be patient. Give before you take, give a lot more than you wish to take. Nature will reciprocate. It never fails.

THE PRICE OF FREEDOM

What is true freedom?

Deep inside, we are free beings. Almost. Even the umbilical cord is snipped at the time of birth to mark our freedom, to sever our ties, to indicate that our primary relationship is with ourselves and not others. Somewhere, even in searching for love that anchors us, we are, in fact, looking for freedom. The more free we feel in a relationship, the more complete we feel. I hear people say, I love this man or woman because I can be myself with him/her. In essence, what we are saying is that *I feel free* when I'm with the one I love.

I've often talked about living freely and fearlessly. I've even used the clichéd *love yourself, be yourself* statements equally frequently. One thing I haven't done though is to shed light on my view of freedom. Does freedom mean you can go out and do anything? Can you or should you make free choices even if it hurts the other person? There truly isn't an absolute answer to these questions, or a guiding principle. It depends from case to case. Having said that, I can certainly share with you how I see freedom. Let me begin with a small story:

A six-year-old boy had to be home alone for a couple of hours. Before leaving, his mother fed him and gave him various instructions related to safety and security. She particularly told him to stay away from the kitchen, the cutlery, etc. Being a good boy, he listened to her attentively, assuring his mother that he well understood what she had said. And yet, being a young boy, he couldn't resist thinking about doing exactly what he had been asked not to do, that is, explore the kitchen.

Soon after his mother left, the boy decided to have some milk and took the milk jug out of the fridge. As he was pouring the milk, it wobbled around the mouth of the jug in a way that half of it was running along the vessel, and some of it was landing inside the glass. He nervously tilted the jug at an odd angle to try and avoid the spill, but ended up losing his grip on the handle altogether! The next moment, the glass jug lay shattered on the ground, with milk splattered all over the floor.

Scared, he ran out of the kitchen and went back to his room. He knew he had messed up but he didn't quite know how to fix it. There was no way of covering up what he had done. In his head, he thought of many excuses, including denying having any knowledge of the incident. But, within him, he knew that it would be very hard to convince his mother.

The mother came home. No sooner had she seen the state of the kitchen, than she confronted her son. The young boy tried one excuse after another. He even said that a ghost scared him when he was trying to pour the milk. The mother kept listening to him for a few minutes and then, holding him by his wrist, pulled him close. Gently, lovingly.

'Everyone makes mistakes, son,' she said. 'Really, we all do. And it's okay. We are free to make mistakes. But we are also responsible for owning up to our actions and accepting our mistakes with grace.'

Thereafter, she asked her son to help her clean up and added, 'If you break the jug, you ought to clean the floor too.'

I call this the price of freedom. The degree of freedom you enjoy in life is directly proportional to your sense of responsibility. The price of freedom is responsibility. The freedom you gain with power, status, wealth, education and so on, lends to your shoulders a responsibility equally great. The more responsible you are, the greater freedom you can have. In the words of Nelson Mandela, 'To be free is not merely to cast off one's chains, but to live in a way that respects and enhances the freedom of others.'

Freedom doesn't mean that just because you are more powerful, you bomb other countries in the face of a conflict, for example. Free speech doesn't mean that you can say whatever comes to your mind. It doesn't mean that you snub the other person just because you can. Freedom, while an immense privilege, is actually an enormous responsibility. True freedom always flourishes in a framework of discipline, it always has an order to it. Always. Freedom without a framework, be it at a personal, social, moral or judicial level, is fatal.

Speaking of freedom, I ought to mention Viktor Frankl's heartrending *Man's Search for Meaning*.[6] Reading this book had moved me to tears. His take on the notion of freedom is most profound, as the following passage will indicate.

> Freedom, however, is not the last word. Freedom is only part of the story and half of the truth. Freedom is but the negative aspect of the whole phenomenon whose positive aspect is responsibleness. In fact, freedom is in danger of degenerating into mere arbitrariness unless it is lived in terms of responsibleness. That is why I recommend that the Statue of Liberty on the East Coast be supplemented by a Statue of Responsibility on the West Coast.
>
> ...
>
> Since Auschwitz we know what man is capable of. And since Hiroshima we know what is at stake.

If we want to move around the kitchen when we shouldn't, we had better learn to handle the jug. And if, by mistake, we break the jug, we ought to take responsibility and leap to damage control.

What good is our freedom if we don't use it to protect someone, to make them feel loved? Of what use is freedom if we choose to hurt the other person just because we can? True freedom is a sense of harmony. And harmony, in a relationship or a society, can't be accomplished unless we act, speak and behave responsibly.

~

A man went for an interview at a Fortune 500 company, for the position of a senior manager.

'Tell us the difference between "complete" and "finished",' the interviewer asked.

It was a tricky question, for a task could be complete and still be unfinished. On the other hand, a task could be finished, and yet be incomplete.

Veering away from conventional management-lingo, the applicant replied, 'If you marry the right woman, you are "complete". If you marry the wrong one, you are "finished".'

He got the job. In fact, that's what freedom is in a nutshell.

When you exercise your freedom correctly, it completes you, it leads to a wholesome outcome. And, when you cloak negligence and indiscretion under the guise of freedom, you destroy the very seed of liberty. You don't feel complete. Instead, you feel restless, maybe even guilty.

Freedom is not I-don't-care-or-whatever-attitude. That's ignorance. True freedom is I-know-what's-at-stake-and-therefore-I'll-act-accordingly.

Be responsible, be free.

HOW TO APOLOGIZE

Can a genuine apology restore another's faith in us?

Fifteen years ago, I was leading a large technology team at a multibillion-dollar media company in Australia. I had just taken over a major portfolio, and a certain issue in the new software was affecting our users and our revenues. As the Tech Lead, it was my responsibility to fix it. We called in many technical experts from various firms but no one could identify the cause. Weeks went by and we made no headway. One time, pensive and introspective, I got home an hour past midnight. I stepped into the shower and had an epiphany. I suddenly knew how to fix the error. I couldn't wait to get back to work and left again after a snooze.

It was during the wee hours of the morning, when I reached office. It was absolutely quiet. I fired up my machine, tried the fix, and voilà! It worked! I bypassed our version control system with great confidence, logged in as the super-user on the staging server. (This was where we showcased our software for business approval before rolling it out for the whole world to see.) I issued a command to clean up the existing directory, so I could copy the new code. I was particularly happy imagining how amazed the exec team would be to come into work in the morning and hear the good news. Here was a simple fix that worked where hundreds and thousands of dollars had failed.

There was a small problem though. And I realized my faux pas, after I started the command on the server. I'd executed a command that was deleting everything (including system files) from the root up. It had effectively formatted the server. Imagine intending to merely turn the light off in your room but ending up cutting the power-supply of your entire town. My action had led to something worse – I'd burnt down the power station too.

It took the hardware team four days to restore the server, for, apparently, there was some issue with the tape-backups too. I was deeply embarrassed. There were many excuses to support my mistake – lack of sleep, pressure at work, ludicrous working hours, cryptic nature of the bug, deficient networking team and so forth, but they were just that, excuses. I offered none. I simply apologized to all the stakeholders. Because, the truth was, I'd made an expensive mistake. Fortunately, it all ended well. Two months later, I got a substantial raise; one of the reasons they offered me one was 'the courage to accept, correct, and learn from the mistake'.

To err is human; we all make mistakes. That, however, can't be the justification to repeat them. There are only two ways to show that we have realized our mistake: first, by not repeating it, and second, by offering a sincere apology. Let's focus on the second point, that is, how to apologize. Apologizing correctly is neither an art nor a craft. It's simply being natural and truthful. When we genuinely regret our action, the right words come out automatically and seeking forgiveness becomes easier.

An apology is restoration of faith. It is conveying that I let you down once, but you can trust me that I won't put you through this again. When we make a mistake, it shakes the trust of the other person. The most positive emotions rest on trust alone. For example, when you love someone, you trust them to be the way you perceive them or the way they project themselves to be. But when they act contrarily, it betrays your trust. This betrayal hurts you, it causes grief, and affects your love and feelings for the other person.

No apology is sincere if you plan on repeating the offence. Think of a broken pot. You can put it together once if you are careful and patient but break it again and the task is a lot more difficult. It is almost impossible. Similarly, when you break someone's trust, they may forgive you once. But if you do it again, you can't reasonably expect them to forget it. Hence, an apology is meaningless if it's insincere. And what is a sincere apology, you may ask?

An apology is genuine when you are determined to not repeat your offence, when you offer no excuse or justification, when you take complete responsibility of your act and when you do so remorsefully. An apology without a sense of remorse is a pointless exercise. In fact, it's going to hurt the other person even more. People often say, 'I'm sorry but I thought this or that…', or, 'I'm sorry but the reason I did it was abc or xyz…', or, 'I'm sorry if my actions hurt you'. These are not apologies, but excuses. Conjunctions like 'if' and 'but' have no room in a true apology. Saying why you did it is no good either.

The best apology is to understand, to feel, to completely accept, and unconditionally at that, that our actions have caused pain to the other person. Don't pollute your apology by citing a reason or a justification, don't ruin it by saying it without meaning it. It'll cause the other person greater pain. You can either choose an apology or an excuse, not both.

A pukka apology is about coming clean and owning up to the offence.

THE NARCISSIST

Do you know what a hot air balloon and a narcissist have in common?

Once, someone sent me the following email:

> *I wanted to ask you how to deal with a narcissistic spouse. How do you deal with them in a spiritual way? When we call someone a narcissist, why are they like that? And, what is the real meaning of narcissist?*

I think a psychologist is better trained to address these questions than a philosopher. Nevertheless, I am happy to share my thoughts on the subject.

I once read a quote: 'That's enough of me talking about myself. Now, let's hear *you* talk about me.' This sums up a narcissistic person.

Think of a very large hot air balloon, bigger than a spaceship. In front of a narcissist's ego, it's no more than a tiny bubble. A narcissist has an insatiable need for admiration and a puffed-up sense of self-importance.

(Many a preacher, swami, religious and political leader fall in this category, by the way.) In most broken relationships, at least one partner strongly displays the traits of a narcissist.

The term narcissism originated from the legend of Narcissus. Born to a river god and a nymph, Narcissus was a strapping and handsome youth, a hunter by profession. He was so enamoured of his own beauty that he even scorned people who loved him because he didn't think anyone was worthy of loving him. Nemesis, the goddess of divine retribution and vengeance in Greek mythology, led Narcissus to a pool where he saw his own reflection and fell in love with himself. He lost the desire to live because he didn't think he could find anyone else as good as the reflection he saw. He stared at his reflection until he died.

Narcissism basically means fixation with oneself.

You asked me how to deal with a narcissistic spouse. The truth is you can't really *deal* with them. You can only take measures to protect yourself. If you are surviving in a relationship with a narcissist, chances are you are too empathetic, too caring. You have put up with a lot, you are being soft and you are hoping your partner will change based on your actions. You are trying to adjust around your spouse's needs hoping he or she won't blow up or hurt you again with their gestures or words. The truth is, these strategies don't really work with a narcissist. They are not the way they are because of you. They are just too self-obsessed.

A narcissist is also an expert manipulator for he or she knows how to extract a certain behaviour from the other person. Even though it's been classified as a disorder, in reality, when it comes to a narcissistic relationship, it's the partner of a narcissist (and not the narcissist himself or herself) who suffers the most. When two narcissists enter into a relationship, they have huge arguments over practically everything. None can take the criticism. They start putting each other down at every opportunity. And eventually they either split up or end up living under the same roof as two complete strangers.

Here are four telltale (or even clear) signs of a narcissist:

1. They can't handle the truth

No matter how constructive your criticism, the only way to deliver it is to absolutely load it with adulation. Even then, if a narcissist is not keen on hearing what you have to say, they'll react undesirably, angrily or even violently. It is nearly impossible to confront a narcissist peacefully. If you have a partner with whom you find it very difficult to communicate, you may have a narcissist at your hands.

2. They are never wrong

If you have a narcissistic spouse, it's always going to be your fault. Period. If he can't get his act together, it's because you didn't do certain things. If he's mad, that's because you set her off. If she is sad, that's because you don't love her enough. If you are having an argument, that's because you don't listen to him or her. A narcissist makes you feel guilty and responsible for his feelings. Somehow, they'll make you feel that you are not doing enough.

3. They always come first

A narcissist has a general lack of empathy for anyone except himself. He or she will have no qualms in grabbing the first plate in a buffet or asking you to take the aisle seat because they want the window. Or, that you dine in a restaurant of their choice or vacation in a destination they prefer. At times, you feel that they are totally indifferent to the feelings, needs and preferences of the other person. They probably are.

4. Their way or the highway

There is rarely any middle path with a narcissistic partner. 'This is how I am,' you'll hear it often. Or, 'This is how I've been brought up.' Or, 'You don't understand me. No one loves me, no one can help me,' etc. By playing the victim, they get their way. Most of the time, they are not doing it intentionally but subconsciously.

A relationship where one partner is a narcissist is generally a broken and an abusive relationship. The amount of mental trauma, stress and conflict you handle on a regular basis in such a relationship is known to you alone. That is because often, a narcissist is unctuous and helpful for the whole world except to his/her partner. So, no outsider can understand what you, as the carer, or the softer partner, are going through.

I'm slightly modifying a joke I once read in Isaac Asimov's *Treasury of Humor*:[7] When you tell a simpleton a joke, he laughs three times. Once when you tell it, next when you explain it and finally when he understands it.

When you tell a landowner a joke, he laughs twice: once when you tell it and once when you explain it.

When you tell a military officer a joke, he laughs only once, when you tell it. He won't let you explain it, and chances are, he doesn't understand it.

But when you tell a narcissist a joke, he tells you that he has heard it before, and that you are telling it all wrong, anyway.

I may have painted a picture that makes narcissists appear like monsters. They are not. No one is. They are fragile human beings, who, beneath their cocky masks, are deeply insecure and vulnerable. Narcissistic behaviour becomes their coping mechanism more than anything else.

If you can't call it quits on your narcissistic partner, there's only one other option left: accept whatever you can and learn to protect yourself. If you can't do that either, you'd better develop infinite compassion, patience and love. This is the spiritual way. Let your goodness rise above your spouse's behaviour. No matter what the circumstances, choose a demeanour that befits you.

As Mahatma Gandhi said, 'I will not let anyone walk through my mind with their dirty feet.' Don't let anyone else's behaviour change yours. The real you, the eternal you, your soul, is beyond all this. No one can hurt you, no one can go there unless you let them. Since you can't change them, emit vibrations of love.

At the end of the day, you should be able to put your hand on your heart and say, 'I did not deter from my path of goodness.' That's all that matters eventually. Like it should.

REALIZING YOUR POTENTIAL

Is there a key to lasting happiness?

In *Tales of the Hasidim,*[8] Martin Buber tells the story of a Jewish master, Rabbi Zusya. The rabbi had led a life of extraordinary devotion and certitude, and yet, when he was dying, he cried inconsolably. Rabbi Zusya's behaviour completely baffled his students who were present in the same room at the time. They tried to pacify him by saying all kinds of positive things, but the rabbi wouldn't stop shedding tears.

'Take heart, Rebbe,' the students spoke, 'you lived an exemplary life. You have been as wise as Moses and as kind as Abraham, so you will be judged positively in heaven.'

'When I go to heaven,' said Zusya, 'I will not be asked why you weren't like Moses, or why you weren't like Abraham. They will ask, why weren't you like Zusya? Why didn't you fully live up to your own potential?'

At the end of the day, that's all that really counts. The question that's of utmost importance is: Have I lived up to my potential? Doing so is not possible, though, unless I have discovered my own truth. Not my teacher's or my ideal's, but my own. And the courage to charter my own course requires self-belief and conviction, neither of which comes unless I'm at peace with myself and my decisions.

I have also realized that to be at peace requires a degree of self-esteem. You must have a certain level of acceptance and love for yourself before you can be at peace with who, where and what you are, figuratively and materially. *And,* it's not possible to love or respect yourself unless you are at ease, unless you live with a sort of carefree abandon. Often, when someone asks us who we are, our first response is to start narrating our CV, that I'm a graduate from such-and-such a university or that I work for so-and-so or that I am the CEO, etc. We rarely say what we stand for. We don't usually say, I'm a kind person, a truthful or an honest person. Instead, we start telling what we do. Such a mindset distances us from the gifts with which we are born. We lose track of why we are here or what we can do with our lives.

Most of us are forever trying to be like someone else. Inspiration is good, imitation, not so. As they say, a true measure of progress is not how well we perform in comparison to others, but how we are doing compared to our own past. As long as comparisons inspire us, it is, perhaps, still healthy. But we are on a perilous road if they make us feel inadequate.

In *Let Your Life Speak: Listening for the Voice of Vocation,*[9] Parker J. Palmer pens down a beautiful passage. I read this book over five years ago, but for some reason the memory of what I had read, especially the gist of his message, has stayed with me. I quote.

> Watching my granddaughter from her earliest days on earth, I was able, in my early fifties, to see something that had eluded me as a twenty-something parent: my granddaughter arrived in the world as *this* kind of person rather than *that*, or *that*, or *that*.
>
> She did not show up as raw material to be shaped into whatever image the world might want her to take. She arrived with her own gifted form, with the shape of her own sacred soul. Biblical faith calls it the image of God in which we are all created... The humanist tradition calls it identity and integrity. No matter what you call it, it is a pearl of great price.
>
> In those early days of my granddaughter's life, I began observing the inclinations and proclivities that were planted in her at birth. I noticed, and I still notice, what she likes and dislikes, what she is drawn toward and repelled by, how she moves, what she does, what she says.
>
> I am gathering my observations in a letter. When my granddaughter reaches her late teens or early twenties, I will make sure that my letter finds its way to her, with a preface something like this: 'Here is a sketch of who you were from your earliest days in this world. It is not a definitive picture – only you can draw that. But it was sketched by a person who loves you very much. Perhaps those notes will help you do

> sooner something your grandfather did only later: remember who you were when you first arrived and reclaim the gift of true self.'

On the battlefield of Kurukshetra, confused about what he ought to do, Arjuna, too, had lost his way. He no longer wanted to be a warrior, or fight for the cause that mattered. He was ready to give up. Krishna gave a similar advice to Arjuna.

> IAST: *śhreyān swa-dharmo viguṇaḥ para-dharmāt sv-anuṣhṭhitāt*
> *svabhāva-niyataṁ karma kurvan nāpnoti kilbiṣham.*
> (Bhagavad Gita 18.47)
>
> You can't give up what comes to you naturally and copy someone else, it's not worth it.
>
> There's no conflict nor confusion when you align your talents with your action.

In my humble opinion, if you choose not to utilize your skills, or make a decision to operate at a level much lower than what you are capable of, you won't experience lasting happiness. Even if we despise it, Nature takes from us work that is in line with our mindset, potential, our stream of consciousness. We may as well then align ourselves for boundless creativity and joy.

Mulla Nasruddin was showing around the newly built university to the chief guest, a local minister, when they stopped by the library with a large inscription that read, 'The Al Habib Hall of Wisdom'.

'Who's Al Habib?' the minister asked curiously. 'Never heard of him!'

'Why, sir,' Mulla replied, 'he was a great author.'

'Really? What did he write?'

'A cheque.'

The world will not remember us for what we kept to ourselves, but what we gave away. We will not be honoured for what we could have done, but what we did. We are not respected for our potential, but our action. We are not valued for the intentions we have, but the outcome we deliver. We don't feel good for what we can do, but for what we actually do. If that's the case, which it is, we may as well reclaim our gifts and do our best. At least, we've got to try. Why just aim for the moon when you can land on it?

THE COSMIC LAW OF INTERCONNECTEDNESS

Is our existence as infinite and eternal as the scriptures claim?

One day, in the court of Empress Wu (624–705 CE), the Chinese monk Fazang (Fa-tsang) was delivering a talk on the Avatamsaka Sutra (lit. the Flower Ornament Sutra). He explained a universe with many dimensions of consciousnesses, many realms of existence that were not just interconnected but mutually contained each other.

'I get it, but I don't get it,' said the Empress. 'I understand interconnectedness, but how can two things contain each other?'

It was common knowledge that the law of interconnectedness was not only the primary but just about the only insight Fazang used in order to make sense of everything around him. He was an eloquent orator and had been engaged by Empress Wu to translate several sutras. Impressed as she was by his versatility, intelligence and, also, political acumen, the Empress had grown increasingly fond of him.

But much as he tried to explain how interconnectedness worked, the Empress remained dissatisfied. 'Can you demonstrate?' she asked, to which Fazang responded that he needed some resources and one week's time.

One evening, seven days later, Fazang invited Empress Wu to a large hall adorned with numerous mirrors. The soft rays of the twilight filtered through large shears and fell on the mirrors, making it an unearthly sight to behold. Right in the middle of that hall was a huge chandelier that sported an unlit candle.

'It feels very calming and surreal to be here,' expressed the Empress.

'With Her Majesty's permission,' Fazang said, 'I'd like to light that candle as soon as the sun goes down fully over the horizon.'

Dusk turned to night, the hall turned dark, the only source of light being the guards standing outside with spears and flambeaus. Fazang lit the candle and asked for the door to be closed.

'Look, Her Majesty,' he said, while taking the Empress around the mirrors, 'simply lighting a single candle illuminates an entire hall. The light of the flame is bouncing off the mirrors, multiplying the effect of that one candle. You see a flame in every mirror. The source flame is only one, but here, it is visible in every mirror. Put out one and all go out.'

'I understand,' the Empress replied, the reflection from the multitudinous flames casting a glimmer in her eyes, and on her jewellery and the goldwork on her dress. 'But, how does that demonstrate things containing each other?'

'Aha!' Fazang exclaimed. 'Please walk with me and observe any mirror carefully.'

'What about it?' she said, standing in front of one.

'Not only does each mirror carry a reflection of the source candle, but it also bears the flame from every other mirror here. Each mirror has infinite flames. This is the law of interconnectedness.'

So it is with us and everyone around us; we are karmically interdependent and interconnected. We carry within ourselves the untold and immeasurable glory of the universe, and eternal impressions of the collective consciousness. What you do, say and think have an impact on others and vice-versa; it creates karma. That's what I mean by collective consciousness – ever-changing and transforming. Buddha called this world *anitya* and *anataman. Anitya* meaning impermanence, and *anataman* denoting the ever-changing nature of the world, devoid of any inherent self. These words encapsulate the gamut of the Buddha's teachings.

Our clinging (*moha*) to our beliefs is nothing but sheer ignorance (*avidya*), a sign of an unawakened mind, a slumbering consciousness. Look at the level of violence, intolerance and unrest in the world today due to people's attachment to their way of life. For that matter, attachment to anything, though natural, stems from ignorance, because the very nature of attachment is the quest for permanence. My beauty, my wealth, my family, youth, status nothing should fade. Attachment hurts us badly whenever we are forced to loosen our grip on the things we wish to retain.

What's worse is that such attachment gives birth to indulgence (*asakti*) and with indulgent behaviour, we sort of develop a mindset that is self-amorous. We become self-absorbed, even self-obsessed. We fall in love with ourselves not in a manner that boosts our self-esteem and ensures our well-being, but in a way that we constantly seek external approval to feel worthy of anything.

If the story ended here, it would still not be so bad. The trouble is that attachment leading to indulgence creates the most destructive of all emotions – *trishna*. The Sanskrit word *trishna* is an incredibly profound word, for it means much more than greed. Just greed is *lobha* in Sanskrit, but *trishna* is that insatiable desire, that futile search for permanence in what is inherently impermanent.

It's all very simple then: with greed, we remain indulgent and attached, which, in turn, keeps the real flame cloaked under the blanket of ignorance. And with ignorance, we continue to cling to whatever we can and as a result, our suffering is endless.

~

A husband called out to his wife from the washroom, 'Honey, can you hand me the towel?'

'Towel!' the wife roared from the kitchen. 'Should I prepare this bloody breakfast for you or give you the towel?'

The man stood there dripping under the shower, which was now turned off.

'First, you always forget the towel and then you leave it on the bed, wet! I have to pick up your dirty laundry, too,' the wife came to the washroom and continued. 'Let alone cleaning the washroom, you leave your shaving gel opened, your razor carelessly facing the top. And then you come out all wet and roam around the house like a bull out of a pond. The other day, our housemaid slipped on the wet floor and did not come for three days. I had to do all the work by myself! Oh God! Why this man!?'

Wonder what my mistake was, the husband thought, to ask for the towel or her hand in marriage?

Maybe the real mistake was his irresponsible behaviour. Or, maybe the wife could be more patient or perhaps they couldn't be bothered. Either way, they'll gradually grow out of love and, one day, wonder, where it all went wrong. Care not about others and the same vibes bounce back at you. A sense of connection fuels interconnectedness.

Have you ever been to a long-awaited vacation with your loved ones, say, to a beautiful hill station? There, let's assume, due to some small misunderstanding, you had an argument or you got some disturbing news from work or whatever. Do you remember how you felt afterwards? The beauty of the mountains, the whiteness of the snow, the singing birds or the gentle brooks, all would have lost their lustre instantly, isn't it? Bereft of any joy inside or outside, you would've been unable to see the beauty. Everything's still there, but it no longer felt that way. That's what ignorance does to our consciousness. It's all there, we just can't see it.

To benefit from the law of interconnectedness, we can't afford to cover the mirror of our consciousness with *trishna* and *svartha,* i.e., self-centredness. They act as a blindfold and prevent us from seeing the flame within the flame, obstructing our vision from seeing the beautiful hall, the sunset, the twilight, that candle in the chandelier. All of that depends on the mirrors being clean and the clarity of your vision.

It is one of the reasons why some people's struggles never abate, they remain on the edge for the most part of their lives. Attachments do that to us; they create noise and turmoil in our heads.

I know what some of you may be thinking, as I'm frequently asked, that should we not have attachment(s) then?

It's not my prerogative to tell you what you can or can't do in your life or what you should or shouldn't have. I don't believe in preaching. Period. All I am saying is that whatever I am attached to will eventually be the cause of my suffering (*dukha*). Without fail. Yes, attachment also motivates us, gives us pleasure, it even strengthens us in a way, but it also makes us oblivious to the truth and the beauty that surrounds us.

The law of interconnectedness is there for everyone, but to have it work for you, one must know how to put the wheels in motion. Someone may have a sum of ten million dollars in their bank account, but if they don't know how to withdraw that money or use it, they can neither spend it nor invest it.

And, how to 'put the wheels in motion', you ask? Be kind. Make a difference to someone's life. Anytime you are hurt, ask yourself, could it be that I'm hurt because I can't see past my viewpoint, maybe because my mirror is covered and I am not seeing the flame that's lit up my whole world? Your inner voice will take over and guide you then to the shores of serenity and love, rekindling a sense of connection with the universe.

Nothing connects like a kind gesture. And, nothing connects forever. The cosmic design just doesn't cater to it.

STORIES WE TELL

Are you telling the wrong stories?

What do you do when someone asks you why you are sad? Usually, you will tell them a story behind your sadness. That so-and-so did or didn't do something for me, or that such-and-such person said xyz to me, or that my life is really difficult, and so on. What's particularly interesting, purely from a psychological perspective, is that we don't view these stories as stories but reasons. We believe we have a legitimate reason for feeling down or sad. Maybe that's true, but mostly it's subjective; these are not the reasons but the stories we tell ourselves.

—

Three bandits looted a family of wayfarers passing through the woods. They killed everyone in the family except the young wife whom they took with them. Late into the night, they got a little drunk and tried to force themselves upon the woman. Knowing she wouldn't be able to free herself out of their grip using force, she played along and served them more liquor. A wee bit later, when they were tipsier and relaxed, she managed to escape unscathed. While trying to get out of the forest, in the pre-dawn hours, she saw the enlightened and serene Mahavira meditating under a tree. The calmness that surrounded him immediately put the young woman at ease.

What a stark contrast, she thought. Here was a man without a thread of clothing on his body, completely naked, and yet he exuded neither desire nor discontent.

'You must be Mahavira,' she said to him, 'the enlightened one of this age, they say. My life is in danger, I seek your refuge.' And the distressed woman narrated the horror of seeing her family get killed by the robbers and her own ordeal.

'I will protect you,' said the sage, and asked her to hide in his thatched hut nearby.

Sure enough, a short while later, the three men came looking for her and stopped to question Mahavira. 'Did you see a young woman pass by?' they asked.

For the awakened, the response to that question couldn't have been a simple yes or no. Saying no would breach his vow of truth and replying in an affirmative would harm the lady.

'A man sees what he wants to see,' Mahavira finally said. 'When I was a man, I saw the woman in every woman, but now, I only see the soul.'

'Just tell us plainly whether you saw her?'

'I've told you already that I only see the soul. You saw me when you arrived but did not notice the trunk of the tree behind me or the branches or the platform I'm sitting on. You only saw what you wanted to see. Give up the ways of violence and lead a life of purity. That's the only way to stop the inflow of karma and the debt it brings.'

The men bowed and went back the way they had come from. What became of them is anyone's guess but legend has it that no more robberies were reported in that region for a long time. It is important to mention that I heard a similar story attributed to the Buddha in one of Osho's discourses. At the end of the day, as far as I'm concerned, it's not about the Buddha or Mahavira, but the message.

And, the words that stood out for me are that a man sees what he wants to see. We all see only that which we choose to see. For instance, you could have a companion on a journey and although you are trying to show them the silent mountains, the flowing rivers, the blue sky and the beauty all around, they may be focused on the carcass of a buffalo. You can't help someone see the world differently unless they are willing to change the story they believe in.

Whether it's another person posing the questions or you asking yourself, it's immaterial, because our story in response remains the same. In other words, if you said to yourself, 'Why am I sad? Why am I disturbed? Why am I unhappy?', in reply, you will tell yourself a story of some kind or another. That the reason you are feeling these things is because you are either lonely or that people haven't been loyal to you or that things haven't gone your way or that you just aren't cut out for this world, etc. The reality, however, may be completely different.

It could be as simple as my refusal to face and accept the truth or align my thoughts with my actions. And the most incredible realization is that it could be any story.

Yes, any at all. It's just a prop, a kind of scaffolding I'm using to climb up and repair the walls of my life. I may as well tell myself a good story then, the kind that inspires and uplifts me.

Mulla Nasruddin opened a hair salon, ready to welcome and serve his customers. Being the first day, a number of people came by, and among them was a man in his early fifties, with a flowing beard.

'Mulla,' he said sheepishly, 'my new wife is coming home today. Just take out all the grey strands from my beard. I must look very young.'

Mulla grabbed a pair of scissors, cut the whole of the man's beard in one snip, and thrusting the hair in his hand, said, 'Here is your beard, *young man*. You can take out the grey hair yourself, I haven't got the time today.'

Taking out the negative incidents from your story can be rather painful and time-consuming. At times, the best solution is to snip it all and have the courage to rewrite your story.

And, if you take a moment to reflect on it, you will discover that we have a story for everything that happens to us. For every single one of our feelings and actions, we tell ourselves a story. That narrative becomes an integral part of our lives; indeed, it takes over our intelligence and wisdom, reducing us to merely a character in the story. Even if that character is the protagonist, it's still just a *part* of the story, whereas you could be the writer of your story. Pen a beautiful one, an inspiring story, as promising as the dreams you carry in your heart.

Leave the horror stories to Stephen King. (Personally, I've never read or watched any works of Stephen King but Vidya Swami has been raving about him lately, so…). Go on, write something full of love and hope.

Oh, and the moral of the story? Change your story if you want to change your life.

LONELINESS

Is there a cure for loneliness?

It's a blessing if you can harness it and be inspired while reveling in it. If not, it is the root cause of persistent restlessness and emptiness. It makes you feel everything is out of place and that you are not complete as an individual or that you must *do* something or find someone and fill the void you are feeling. Maybe you need to be in a new or a different relationship, perhaps you need to change your job or move to a new country, or who knows, you may just be depressed. That feeling of falling in an abyss or just staring at a wall not knowing where you are heading or ought to go, all of that stems from one's inability to handle it. By 'it', I mean loneliness.

Loneliness is what you experience when you feel utterly directionless in your life, when you find everything pointless (even if for a short while). It is remarkable how an increasing number of people are being plagued and pestered by feelings of intense loneliness.

I had once read an interesting passage in Matt Haig's *Notes on a Nervous Planet*:[10]

> Have you ever heard a parent moan about their kids' need for constant entertainment?
>
> You know, 'When I was young I could sit in the back of the car and stare out the window at clouds and grass for 17 hours and be perfectly happy. Now our little Misha can't go five seconds in the car without watching Alvin and the Chipmunks or playing game apps or taking selfies of herself as a unicorn…' That sort of thing.
>
> Well, there is an obvious truth to it. The more stimulation we have, the easier it is to feel bored.
>
> And this is another paradox.
>
> In theory, it has never been easier to not be lonely. There is always someone we can talk to online. If we are away from loved ones, then we can Skype them. But loneliness is a feeling as much as anything. When I have had depression, I have been lucky enough to have people who love me all around me. But I had never felt more alone.
>
> I think the American writer Edith Wharton was the wisest person ever on loneliness. She believed the cure for it wasn't always to have company, but to find a way to be happy with your own company. Not to be antisocial, but not be scared of your own unaccompanied presence.
>
> She thought the cure to misery was to 'decorate one's inner house so richly that one is content there,

> glad to welcome anyone who wants to come and stay, but happy all the same when one is inevitably alone'.

I couldn't agree more. Just like fulfilling your desires gives birth to more desires, trying to fill loneliness by having company does not really work in the longer run. I am not denying that human interaction, companionship, community and so on, are essential to our well-being. They cannot, however, be the centre of your life without great personal inconvenience. Socializing and all may help you diminish your feelings of aloneness, or momentarily make you forget about how lonely you actually are, but at the end of the day, they won't let you get past your loneliness.

Majority of the self-help books say that an absence of a passion in life makes you lonely. That, if you are feeling lonely, chances are you don't have any plausible reason to live or go on in your life. There's perhaps nothing that excites you to wake up before your alarm goes off in the morning and so on. Hence, common wisdom says fill your life with something or someone.

From a yogic perspective, these are still temporary measures. I can be passionately crazy about something or someone, but that does not mean I won't feel lonely. Look at some of the most successful artists and musicians who breathed and lived their art, and yet, slipped into depression. Yoga says that loneliness is a beautiful opportunity to explore yourself, to reflect on not just what you can do but what you have done. When you maintain mindfulness in loneliness, you discover this vast reservoir of calm and peace. If anything, loneliness is a calling of the soul.

Intense awareness in great loneliness is nothing short of nirvana. In ordinary loneliness, you are simply flowing with your thoughts and feelings that are often negative when unchecked. In a more pristine form of loneliness, which I refer to as yogic loneliness or solitude of the mind, you maintain acute awareness of every little thought, of each passing moment. You begin to realize that you are truly unborn, undying, unalloyed, that you are beyond the ageing body you wear or the chattering mind you carry.

The wisdom of life begins to dawn on you in such quiet moments. All those you love or hate, want or detest, crave or avoid, these people including yourself are here for only a short period.

> IAST: *avyaktādīni bhūtāni vyakta-madhyāni bhārata avyakta-nidhanāny eva tatra kā paridevanā.*
>
> (Bhagavad Gita 2.28)
>
> 'What are you grieving about O Arjuna!' said Krishna. 'These people did not exist in the past, they will cease to be in the future. Just for a little while now that you are here, they are there in your life. What's the attachment then?'

Everyone we meet in our lives is on their own individual journey; we simply cross paths. The cure for loneliness, therefore, is not to find someone or something that keeps you engaged, happy or busy. It is but to find your centre of awareness and realize that to taste lasting happiness, we must turn inward and embrace the beauty of loneliness.

Yogic texts called such loneliness supremely liberating. They gave it the term *kaivalya*: you in your own company basking in utter peace and absorption. Due to our conditioning, desires and actions, there exists a chasm between the intellect and the soul. With self-enquiry, reflection and mindfulness, this gap begins to close, and as that occurs, it brings you closer to you.

> IAST: *sattva-puruṣayoḥ śuddhisāmye kaivalyam iti.*
>
> (Yoga Sutras of Patanjali 3.55)
>
> Thus, when the purity of intellect equals the purity of soul, one reaches the final state of emancipation...

~

A beautiful girl was drinking coffee in a café when Mulla Nasruddin approached her.

'Are you alone?' he asked her, with an unmistakeable shyness in his voice.

'I've been alone for a long time,' she sighed.

'In that case, may I take this chair?'

If you are seeking someone in your life because you are lonely, you will be disappointed. You are seeking a seat in their heart and they, perhaps, simply want your chair. Granted that having another person will keep you busy as most worldly relationships do, but busyness does not equal fulfilment or bliss. Two lonely people do not make a festive crowd.

When you simplify and declutter your life, when you devote time to the well-being of your mind and soul, when you live in harmony with feelings of love and kindness towards all sentient beings, you bridge the gap between your intellect and soul.

Walking past your conditioned intellect, you realize that you are beyond all that grieves you, far above all that you crave, that you are not just a shining star in the universe but the universe itself. Who can then make you feel lonely or snap you out of loneliness? No one. If anyone, only one person wields the power to pull you out of your loneliness once and for all. And that person is you. The complete you, the beautiful you, the indestructible you that is seated in you, that being of boundless glory and magnificence, who is forever away from anything even remotely close to ordinary loneliness.

The only true and eternal relationship you have is with *your* self. Live it. Love it. Value it. It's worth it.

A THOUSAND MARBLES

What comes first: work or family?

A few years back, I had read a story and made a mental note to use it someday. Here it is, almost as I had read it:[11]

> The older I get, the more I enjoy Saturday mornings. Perhaps it's the quiet solitude that comes with being the first to rise, or maybe it's the unbounded joy of not having to be at work. Either way, the first few hours of a Saturday morning are most enjoyable.
>
> A few weeks ago, what began as a typical Saturday morning turned into one of those lessons that life seems to hand you from time to time.
>
> I was listening to my favorite Saturday program on radio where listeners would call in and share their issues and so on. And besides the host, other callers could also offer their perspective. Someone by the name of Tom made a call and shared how he had to stay away from his family due to the nature

of his work but that the job paid him really well and that he was having the time of his life. He was thirty-two years old and his question was: what should his priority be – job or family?

Another listener called in, an older sounding chap with a golden voice. You know the kind, he sounded like he should be in the broadcasting business himself. He offered some advice I would never forget.

'Well, Tom,' he said, 'it sure sounds like you're busy with your job. They must pay you well but it's a shame you have to be away from home and your family so much. Hard to believe a young fellow should have to work sixty or seventy hours a week to secure his future.

'Let me tell you something that has helped me keep a good perspective on my own priorities,' the old man continued. 'My theory of a thousand marbles. You see, I sat down one day and did a little arithmetic. The average person lives about 75 years. I know, some live more and some live less but on average, folks live about 75 years.

'Now then, I multiplied 75 times 52 and I came up with 3900 which is the number of Saturdays that the average person has in their entire lifetime. It took me until I was fifty-five years old to think about all this in any detail and by that time I had lived through over 2800 Saturdays. I got to thinking that if I lived to be 75, I only had about 1100 of them left to enjoy.

'So, I went to a toy store and bought every single marble they had,' the old man went on. 'I ended up with 1000 marbles. I took them home and put them inside a large clear plastic container next to the radio. Every Saturday since then, I have taken one marble out and thrown it away. I found that by watching the marbles diminish, I focused more on the really important things in life. There is nothing like watching your time here on this earth run out to help get your priorities straight.

'Now let me tell you one last thing before I sign off with you and take my lovely wife out for breakfast. This morning, I took the very last marble out of the container. I figure if I make it until next Saturday then I have been given a little extra time. And the one thing we can all use is a little more time. I hope you spend more time with your loved ones. Have a good morning!'

You could have heard a pin drop when he finished. Even the show's moderator didn't have anything to say for a few moments. I had planned to do some work that morning, then go to the gym. Instead, I went upstairs and woke my wife up with a kiss. 'C'mon honey, I'm taking you and the kids to breakfast.'

'What brought this on?' she asked with a smile.

'Oh, nothing special, it's just been a long time since we spent a Saturday together with the kids.'

She jumped out of bed in excitement.

'Plus,' I said to her, 'I need to buy some marbles.'

Most of us today are driven by work, goals, ambition and so on. We feel that we'll lose the edge if we don't stay on top of everything and there's this fear of missing out (FOMO) which forces us to stretch ourselves beyond what we can reasonably do. We do it at the cost of our health, spiritual and physical well-being, and at the expense of things that really matter to us. I'm not denying that the world is uber-competitive, but if you look around those who lead a more balanced life, they are growing and doing just fine.

In a hospice in the US they did a survey once and asked terminal patients about their greatest regret in life. Not even one of those patients said they wished they'd spent more time working or if they could have finished that important thesis or launched a certain product. Every single one wrote how dearly they wished to go back in time and spend more time with their family.

Repeatedly, scriptures remind us that everything is impermanent, that none of this is going to last. Whatever we have right now in our lives, won't be there one day. Some Saturday certainly is going to be our last Saturday. There'll be a morning when we won't wake up, a moment after which we won't breathe again. No one can escape that. Considering that this is the irrefutable truth, realizing that everything is impermanent, isn't it all the more reason to live our lives fully? Certainly, working all the time is not leading a full life. Busy, yes; full, no. It is so easy to get distracted and lose sight of our priorities. Even a simple distraction like Candy Crush Saga can have you spend hours and hours doing something that has no bearing on anything.

All those hours that you could have spent in the gym, in a garden, with your loved ones, or even just resting, got spent on a worthless pursuit. The reason? Lapse of mindfulness.

I think it is a brilliant idea to calculate how many Saturdays are left before you'll turn 75 (or 77) and then put as many marbles in a clear jar. Take one out each Saturday. As the wise man said on the radio, 'There is nothing like watching your time here on this earth run out to help get your priorities straight.' This could be your jar of life or simply the jar of mindfulness. Turn FOMO into JOMO (Joy of Missing Out). We don't have to know everything that's going on in the world, we don't have to read all the literature out there or be on top of everything. Just take it easy.

Mulla Nasruddin had a friend over at his house and his wife decided to feed their guest hot chapatis with nice curries. One by one Mulla brought him chapatis fresh off the stove until his friend said he was full.

'Have one more!' Mulla insisted.

'No, Mulla,' he replied. 'I already had five!'

'Not that I usually count but you actually ate seven chapatis.'

Whether anyone is counting or not, a record is being kept. No, I am not saying that someone is sitting up there somewhere with a ledger. It's just that each one of us is inching towards that final moment. It's not worth it to waste our time on petty emotions, resentment, on just material goals. You may work very hard all your life so you may live by the beach for a few years after you've retired. Eventually, you will be in a room in the city with your children or in an aged-care where you may have a garden view at the most. To destroy your present in the hope of a better future could hardly be a wise strategy. Your today was your future yesterday. Future is not a distant date or a final destination. It's here already, the next step.

We often forget where we should be spending our time. We try to impress those who don't matter with things we don't own. We work on things we don't want so we may earn to spend on things we don't need. I doubt if this is how you dreamed your life would unfold when you were a child. It needn't be this way. We worry about stuff that is completely irrelevant in the larger scheme of things … *whereas you do not know what will happen tomorrow! What is your life? It is even a vapour that appears for a little time and then vanishes away* (James, 4:14).

Slow down, pause. Stop. Is this what you really want to be doing? Which path you wish to walk is entirely your prerogative. Just be mindful.

III SELF

THE TEARING THOUGHT

What to do when the wild elephant of thoughts tears into your garden of peace and quiet?

Has it ever happened to you that you are unable to shake off a certain thought or feeling? In fact, it happens to most of us more frequently than we might care to count. Everything is going fine and then out of the blue, some negative thought runs amok in our mind like an elephant gone wild, razing our peace and calm in practically no time.

We sit wondering why I'm feeling like this or that I don't want to think these thoughts or feel these things. These thoughts that completely derail us while we helplessly watch our own destruction is a common scenario in every person's life. During these moments, meditation, wisdom, affirmations, etc., simply go for a toss and only one thing rules the universe of our mind: a tearing thought.

Is there any method to handle a tearing thought, that gatecrasher who barges into our consciousness? Yes. That's the good news. The bad news? It isn't exactly a piece of cake. How do we rise above such thoughts then?

First, let me share with you a beautiful story, one I had come across in Thich Nhat Hanh's *Being Peace*.[12] I once cited it in one of my discourses, too.

The Buddha once told a story about a young man who was a trader and had a beautiful wife and baby boy. Sadly, his wife fell ill and died, and the man poured all his love into his little child, who became the sole source of his happiness and joy.

Once, while he went away on business, bandits raided his village, burned it to the ground and captured his five-year-old son. When he returned and saw the devastation, he was beside himself with grief. He found the charred corpse of a small child, and in his desperation, he took it for the body of his son. He tore at his hair and beat his chest, weeping uncontrollably.

At last, he arranged a cremation ceremony, collected the ashes, and put them in a pouch made of very precious silk. Whether he was working, sleeping or eating, he always carried that bag of ashes with him. And often, he would sit alone and weep for hours.

One day, his son escaped from the bandits, and found his way home. It was midnight when he arrived at his father's new house and knocked on its door. The man was in bed, sobbing, the bag of ashes by his side.

'Who is it?' he asked.

The child answered, 'It's me, daddy, it's your son. Open the door.'

In his anguish and confusion, all that the father could think of was that some malicious boy was playing a cruel trick on him.

'Go away,' he shouted, 'leave me alone.' Then he started to cry once more.

Again and again the boy knocked, but the father refused to let him in. Finally, he turned back slowly and walked away. The father and son never saw one another ever again.

When he came to the end of his story, the Buddha said, 'Sometime, somewhere you take something to be the truth. But if you cling to it too strongly, then even when the truth comes in person and knocks on your door, you will not open it.'

There are two important aspects of a nagging thought that ruins our peace. First is the thought itself and second, our overactive imagination. Dropping a thought is a practice in meditation that can be learned and cultivated. Once you master it, all you have to do is to hold a mini self-dialogue and gently shift your attention to something positive.

An overactive imagination, on the other hand, is more like a spiritual disorder. It's similar to excessive or compulsive thinking. When we start to imagine stuff, the thought starts to inflate like a balloon and usurps our entire mind. Soon, the only thing we see, think, hear, observe is everything linked to that thought. And even when something is not connected, your mind will just link it anyway. That becomes our truth. It starts to govern our attitude and behaviour towards everything in life. Fears, phobias, anxiety and other noxious emotions fill our minds.

Lingering thoughts and feelings usually come in waves. Where an average person is constantly tossed about, a good meditator learns to surf these waves. The first thing about a tearing thought is to recognize it the moment it appears. Without such mindfulness, it is impossible to move away from that thought and shift our attention elsewhere. I would like to add that I didn't coin this insightful term: tearing thought. I first came across it in *The Yoga of Kashmir Shaivism*[13] by Swami Shankarananda. Here's what he writes about these thoughts:

> I often refer to tearing thoughts. These are thoughts that attack us, like 'I am weak. I am worthless. I am no good. That other person is better than I am.' Tearing thoughts are an extraordinary psychological phenomenon. When cells take the wrong path and start to attack the organ they live in, we call it cancer. Tearing thoughts are a kind of autoimmune failure of the mental body.
>
> The mind, which should be used for our benefit – solving problems, understanding issues, writing poetry – instead turns against us with devastating effect. Enemies are insignificant when our own minds tear into us.
>
> If there is a single phenomenon that epitomizes being deluded by your own energies, it is tearing

> thoughts. A tearing thought is a terrorist who has already penetrated your deepest defense system and lives in your hometown with vile intentions. If you could stop this one tendency you would be entirely transformed. When we have a failure in life, it is not so much the defeat that brings us down, but what we take it to mean about ourselves. We say, 'Oh I lost that game, therefore I'm worthless'. We have a tantrum, we take to our beds, we make everyone suffer for miles around. The one who suffers most is us. If we didn't have tearing thoughts, we would simply say, 'Now what can I learn from that? That's good, I'll do that next time'. And we move on cleanly and clearly.
>
> If you are successful in some aspect of your life and if you examine your inner process, you will discover that you are not afflicted by tearing thoughts in that area. We defeat ourselves by getting caught in the pernicious downward spiral of tearing thoughts.

When we accept the cyclical nature of our life and thoughts, we ease up a bit. We start to realize that not everything in life can happen the way I want. Not all my dreams will come true, that the universe has its own plans too. Once we get a handle on it, the rest is easy. It's no rocket science. Here's my personal recipe of life that will help you keep tearing thoughts at bay. Consume it daily and share it with others.

The Om Swami Pudding for Top Mental and Spiritual Health			
Common Name (What you hear)		Yogic Name (What I really mean)	Quantity
1	Compassion	Stop doing me-me-me.	1 cup
2	Meditation	Learn to be silent.	½ cup
3	Gratitude	Stop complaining.	3 cups
4	Purpose	Stop being lazy and do something with your life.	4 cups
5	Words	If you can't speak gently and nicely, better keep quiet.	4 cups
6	Charity	Learn to share.	As per taste
Cooking Time: Lifetime			
Enough to serve the whole world.			

There's no one singular prayer, meditation or method that can help you keep your mind at peace under all circumstances. Life must be savoured the way it comes. There are some things we can change, but a lot of it is about our attitude towards life, which dictates our behaviour and choice of words in any situation. And our attitude, in turn, is determined by our mindset and beliefs. Mindset can be changed with meditation, wisdom and inspiration. Beliefs can be changed with education, experience and insight.

In the dead of night, a man had to pass through a cemetery. Much to his horror and awe, he heard music coming out of a grave. Someone was playing a famous symphony of Mozart backwards. Shocked, he picked up speed to get out of there but ran into the caretaker.

'Good lord!' the man stuttered in fear. 'That grave ... that grave ... I hear music coming out of that grave.'

'Any surprise?' said the caretaker. 'That's Mozart buried right there!'

'So, his spirit is playing reverse piano or something? This is so spooky.'

'Take it easy, man,' the caretaker replied. 'He's just decomposing.'

Our thoughts and feelings compose us, and our actions and words decompose us. What we play in our actions and speech is merely what we have known in our thoughts and emotions. If you feed your mind and heart with noble thoughts and feelings, your mindset and beliefs will turn noble automatically. This leads to transformation of one's attitude. The six ingredients of the divine pudding will easily subdue a pinch of tearing thought. Garnish it with a smile. Be noble.

SHEDDING YOUR PAST

How can one get over the gnawing guilt?

'I want to change but my past haunts me, Swami,' a visitor once said to me.

'I constantly feel guilty for my sins. How do I get rid of my baggage?'

'Two things will follow you to your grave,' I replied. 'Wanna guess?'

'My karma?'

'And creditors,' I joked. 'One comes with baggage and the other with a bag.'

He laughed a nervous laugh.

'One is debt,' I added, 'and the other a debt-collector.'

Our baggage is our unpaid debt. And in our lives, we attract all sorts of people, some of whom are karmic creditors and they play the role of debt-collectors. That is not to say that there's no way of shedding our past.

Out of ignorance or arrogance, we all seem to have said or done things we wish we hadn't. Doing bad karma does not necessarily make one bad though. Often, good people end up doing bad things and the so-called bad people do plenty of good, too. A mere bad thought or action does not make you inferior. Instead, what reveals inferiority of consciousness is when we don't have the courage to admit that, yes, I messed up and I am sorry about it.

Denial or non-admission of our mistakes creates more baggage than anything else. The moment we gracefully accept our fault, we flush out of our system the emotions of anger (why did I have to be in that situation?) and guilt (why couldn't I act differently?). No doubt that the incident may remain etched on your mind for a long time, but its recollection does not wreck your peace any more.

In *The Way of Chuang Tzu*,[14] Thomas Merton cites a beautiful story called 'Flight from Shadow':

> There was a man who was so disturbed by the sight of his own shadow and so displeased with his own footsteps that he was determined to get rid of both. The method he hit upon was to run away from them.
>
> So he got up and ran. But every time he put his foot down there was another step, while his shadow kept up with him without the slightest difficulty.
>
> He attributed his failure to the fact that he was not running fast enough. So he ran faster and faster, without stopping until he finally dropped dead.
>
> He failed to realize that if he merely stepped into the shade, his shadow would vanish, and if he sat down and stayed still, there would be no more footsteps.

Call it our past, baggage, our shadow or anything else, the fact is we can't really undo our actions. We can't take back words we have already uttered or our undesirable actions. At the most, we can apologize, repent, regret or even heal over time. The truth remains that our past travels with us wherever we go. Only when we are in darkness, does our shadow merge with it. In such darkness, we may momentarily feel that we have no baggage, but that's an illusion, because we have not gotten rid of the darkness. Instead, we have hidden ourselves from light.

Even the most luminous of rooms has a dark corner, however small it maybe. Similarly, even the best-lived life hides in its heart a darkness of some kind. That's our shadow, we can't get rid of it and we have absolutely no reason to be afraid of it. We are beings of light and, therefore, this shadow is inseparable from our existence. What matters is not how long or dark our shadow is, but where it is: in front of us or behind us.

One way to have respite from your shadow, as Chuang Tzu contended, is to step into the shade. The tree of grace has that shade as does the tree of truth and forgiveness. The shade these trees offer softly absorbs the shadow of the person underneath it.

Another way, often tempting, is to be in the dark and live in it. In darkness, while you may not see the shadow, you won't see much else either … no beauty, no light. Millions around us choose to shut themselves from everyone and everything. Out of fear, paranoia, guilt and other feelings, they spend an entire lifetime in the dark just to avoid a shadow. The wise one, however, knows better.

It's only when our shadow is in front of us that the path ahead appears dark. When our shadow is ahead of us, we turn our back towards light. When you walk towards light, your shadow will go behind you. It will no longer obscure your path with darkness.

And that's just about the only method I know of dropping our baggage: we must journey towards light with hope and compassion for ourselves and others. This is the only means by which to leave our shadow behind us. Forgive yourself for the mistakes of the past. Go easy. This will do you much good and will help you do good for others, which in the longer run, can only ever be a good thing.

If you keep walking, your footprints will be behind you. Stop and brood, and you are right on them. Pretending that we are spotless like the fresh Himalayan snow, at some point in time, each one of us has cast stones at others. At times, we have been at the receiving end, too. In the end, it does not matter much so long as we put it behind us.

~

Here's a nice joke I came across in Imam Jamal Rahman's *The Comic Teachings of Mulla Nasruddin and Other Treasures*, which I have edited slightly. A mother brought her rude young son to Mulla, complaining that she was tired of his rebellious ways.

'Please,' she said, 'do something to put a little fear in his heart.'

'Right away,' Mulla said confidently. 'He'll be docile as a cow in no time.'

Mulla stared fiercely into the boy's eyes and commanded him to listen to his mother. He contorted his face terribly and growled deeply. The whole act was so fearsome that the mother fainted and Mulla rushed out of the room. When she regained consciousness, she chided Mulla. 'I asked you to frighten my son, not me!'

'Madam,' Mulla replied, 'when you invoke fear, it consumes everyone. It has no favourites. Why, I got so scared myself that I had to leave the room.'

Our shadow, like fear, has no personal favourites. Wherever a shadow falls, a hue of darkness arises naturally. That's why it's all the more important that we not only make a commitment to face and walk into light, but also inspire others to do the same. For we may be as bright as the mid-day sun, but if people around us are living in darkness, their shadows will fall on our paths. Be the light and spread light. Moving in the direction of a noble aspiration, towards goodness and kindness, is like walking into the light.

Let the light of the heart merge with the infinite light around you. Darkness will not matter then. If anything, it will only give greater depth, purpose and meaning to your life.

Keep walking ... towards light.

WHOM TO PLEASE

Is it possible for two people to be in love, be together and yet be on different paths?

The other day a young man asked me innocently, 'Whom should I please? There are my parents, siblings, wife, children, boss and others. How should I choose between them? Or do I try and keep everyone happy?'

'You forgot the most important person,' I said.

'God?'

'You.'

Eventually, happiness in our daily lives depends on how happy I'm able to keep myself and others, neither of which is easy. Please note the word 'eventually'. In the short term, you can make a lot of sacrifices and keep everyone happy. But as time wears on, this will leave you weak and unfulfilled. And forget everyone, even to keep yourself happy is particularly tricky because no matter how talented, skilled or successful you are, regardless of how many hobbies you may have to keep yourself busy – you can't keep yourself happy all the time on your own.

Unless, of course, you have mindfully and compassionately dissociated yourself from the world and turned inwards, in which case you'll be happier than most people. My focus is on people living in the real world with real challenges, where we undergo a whole range of emotions on a daily basis.

Have you noticed that whenever we are suffering, it's generally due to the presence or absence of someone else in our life? We are sad because we have the wrong person in our life or we are sad because the right person is no more (or not as much as we'd like them to be) in our life. (What have we reduced ourselves to? I wonder…)

The newly elected prime minister went to a mental institution to show that he cared about everybody.

'What's wrong with this man?' he asked the warden about a man, who was alternating between wailing and laughing.

'Sir, he was in love but his girlfriend ran off with somebody else. As a result, he had a major nervous breakdown and he went mad.'

'That's very sad,' the prime minister said sympathetically and moved on to see other patients.

A block later, he saw another person who was acting most weirdly. 'And, what happened to him?'

'This is the man, sir,' the warden replied, 'whom she ran off with and married.'

We go mad in happiness as we do in sadness (figuratively, generally). Relationships are difficult, and loneliness can be even more difficult. Primarily because you can't resolve loneliness by entering into a relationship. It's not the opposite of togetherness. People can be incredibly lonely even when surrounded by their loved ones. Loneliness is difficult because it's a feeling of isolation, you've become distanced from yourself; others have little or nothing to do with it. Having said that, most people are lonely for the lack of quality in their relationships. They tried, maybe they tried very hard, but something was amiss, it just didn't work out.

Usually, it's all fireworks in the beginning and then gradually it loses its charm, like new cutlery that's shiny and sparkly clean in the beginning and then suddenly, one day, after a while, you find that it's looking old, it's lost its sheen. Loneliness bites you the most when you don't want to be lonely. You get a promotion and you want to call someone to celebrate, for someone to partake of your happiness; or if you just got fired, once again, you want to share your sorrow with someone. Whether we suffer out of loneliness or togetherness, it's often because we miss having a quality relationship with someone. Quality is the key. What do I mean by quality and how to have a quality relationship?

I came across a nice little write-up in Nassim Taleb's *The Bed of Procrustes*.[15]

> Procrustes, in Greek mythology, was the cruel owner of a small estate in Corydaluys in Attica, on the way between Athens and Eleusis, where the mystery rites were performed. Procrustes had a peculiar sense of hospitality (if we might call it that): he abducted travelers, provided them with a generous dinner,

then invited them to spend the night in a rather special bed. He wanted the bed to fit the traveler to perfection. Those who were too tall had their legs chopped off with a sharp hatchet; those who were too short were stretched.

In the purest of poetic justice, Procrustes was hoisted by his own petard. One of the travelers happened to be the fearless Theseus, who, after the usual dinner, made Procrustes lie in his own bed. Then, to make him fit in it to the customary perfection, he decapitated him.

...

We humans, facing limits of knowledge, and things we do not observe, the unseen and the unknown, resolve the tension by squeezing life and the world into crisp commoditized ideas, reductive categories, specific vocabularies, and prepackaged narratives, which, on the occasion, has explosive consequences. Further, we seem unaware of this backward fitting, much like tailors who take great pride in delivering the perfectly fitting suit – but do so by surgically altering the limbs of their customers.

I guess so are most relationships: a kind of Procrustean bed. We work very hard to make the other person want the same things as us. We mistakenly want to work our relationships into some sort of perfection. If that is how you intend to make any relationship work, I'm afraid, it never will. The quality of human bond is not based on how well two people fit together or just even fit in. Instead, it is

> how much space they give each other. Besides, often when they seem to get along like a house on fire, one of them is quietly smoldering. Freedom is the seed of quality in a relationship.

By freedom, I don't just mean that you are able to do whatever you want to do. In fact, such irresponsible freedom is the termite that hollows even the best of relationships.

Freedom to me is respecting co-existence. It is as much about celebrating togetherness as it is about respecting diversity, a sort of fearlessness. In other words, it is maturity. You can't have a free relationship unless two people are mature enough to voice their concerns, desires and truth. A bond devoid of such maturity will leave both feeling burned out.

I read somewhere once, 'We must know that every person in the world has his own object in life, his own interest and his point of view, and that he is concerned with himself. His peace is disturbed when you wish to interest him in your object of interest. If you wish to force upon him your point of view, however near and dear he may be to you, he is not pleased with it.'

Though it may sound too categorical to be real in our world full of relative happiness, it is the uncomfortable truth of human existence: we are too concerned with ourselves. We are told to share, be good and all that, but at the same time, we are taught to watch out for ourselves. Even my advice to the young man was that he didn't count himself in his pursuit of happiness because you are an important part of *your* life. However, if there's too much emphasis on winning, on being right, then I'm set to be disappointed repeatedly, for no matter how capable I may be, my losses will outnumber my wins. And, that's where the question of delicate balance arises.

I must be clear about what's the minimum I require from my life and what's the best I can do for the other person. Maturity is when two people can sit down, negotiate and work through things. Understanding arises when they acknowledge and respect the fact that each one of them has the right to choose their own object in life. And more importantly, a different path does not mean that you don't love the other person. That, in fact, is the hallmark of true maturity, where you don't equate everything in terms of what it means for or to you.

There's bound to be fulfilment and a sense of togetherness in a mature relationship for you know that you can share your joys and sorrows without being judged or reprimanded. That, there's freedom and understanding. Then, the question of how or who you should please disappears. Moving from the depths of your heart, the joy of sharing rises to the brim.

~

A priest called in sick on a Sunday and went to play golf. All by himself. He wanted to improve his swing for the upcoming friendly tournament. He knew well that his golfing skills were nothing to write home about.

Most miraculously though, that day, no matter how he hit the ball, it would end up in the hole. Indeed, the ball that was flying south would turn north and land in the hole.

The priest jumped up and down in sheer joy. With sixteen holes-in-one, he swelled with pride like fresh popcorn.

'Why?' an angel asked God, who had been observing all this for two hours. 'Why did you help a priest who skipped his duty to play golf? Shouldn't he be punished? Instead, he plays the best golf of his life!'

'Well,' God replied, smilingly, 'who's he gonna tell?'

Doesn't one of the greatest joys of our lives lie in being able to share our successes and achievements with our loved ones? Just as it's most comforting to share your failings with the person whom you expect to hear you out non-judgementally? That cannot come unless there's maturity in a relationship. Maturity, in turn, is not possible without responsible freedom. And, freedom is a synonym of true love. If you want to tie the other person down, dictate rules for how they should lead their life (no matter how reasonable or moral those rules might appear to you), that kind of togetherness leads to suffocation.

And when that happens, it has the opposite effect: it's no longer their absence but presence that makes you feel lonely. Sometimes, all it takes to fix it is to sit down and ask each other, 'What would make you happy?' Thereafter, negotiate what's doable. If there's maturity, coming to a common ground is a good possibility. And, if maturity is missing, well then, as it is, such a relationship has little meaning. A fallout is only a matter of time then.

Maturity comes naturally in love, like warmth in the winter sun. All else is an illusion of love; perhaps it is attachment. Take it easy. Work it through.

WHAT I COULD HAVE DONE

What should we do when someone tries to harm us?

Very often people ask me what they should do when someone does bad to them. Or how they should act when they find themselves in difficult circumstances having to do things they would rather not. Every time I'm posed these questions, I'm reminded of a beautiful story I read in *Three Times Chai*[16] by Laney Katz Becker, a book presenting the Jewish tradition of storytelling. It was a story that talked about a devout Christian who was involved with the Danish underground, an organization that rescued a large number of Jews in Denmark from the Nazi pogrom.

> Jordan Knudsen was an ambulance driver. He was also an active member of the Danish underground during World War II. The underground had just learned of the day when the SS (the Schutzstaffel, the Nazis' elite defense force) was planning to begin deporting Denmark's Jews to the death camps.

This news served as the signal for the underground to spring into action.

Being an ambulance driver in a totalitarian system was (and remains) an extraordinarily valuable occupation because an ambulance driver can turn on the vehicle's siren and go almost anywhere. Since Knudsen drove an ambulance, he had an ideal means by which to smuggle Jews out of the country. But he had a problem, and it wasn't insignificant: He didn't know anyone who was Jewish. There were seventy-five hundred Jews in the country, and he didn't know a single one of them. So – what to do?

Knudsen could have done nothing – how many people in a similar position would have chosen that option? But he was determined to do something. So, he found a telephone directory and flipped through its pages, looking for names that struck him as Jewish. Knudsen knew that certain names were frequently Jewish. Once he came across a listing with a Jewish-sounding name, he drove to the corresponding address. If Jews were living there, he took them in his ambulance to a hospital, which was the first step in smuggling the Jews into neutral Sweden, where they could survive the war in safety.

Many years after World War II ended, researchers at Yad Vashem (an organization safeguarding the memory of Holocaust victims) found Knudsen and interviewed him.

They asked him, 'Why did you do it? After all, if you'd been caught, you would have been killed.

> You risked your life, and you didn't even know anyone you helped. You didn't even know anyone who was Jewish.'
>
> His answer was extraordinary in its simplicity: 'What else could I have done?' That's all he said.
>
> Knudsen's response was particularly haunting considering that those were the exact words used by the Nazis in their defense at Nuremberg. When the officers and other members of the SS responsible for the systematic murdering of millions of Jews were questioned individually at the trial, that why did they support Hitler, they'd answered, 'What else could I have done?'

As I always say, under all circumstances, act in a manner that befits you. For that matter, we all act according to our inherent nature, which determines our knee-jerk reactions in most situations. Such reactions or our spontaneous actions are largely influenced by our subconscious mind. And, our subconscious mind, I may add, is a giant storehouse of our past thoughts, experiences and emotions. In a way, this question of what-should-you-do-when-someone-does-bad-to-you becomes redundant because you're most likely to do whatever comes naturally to you.

Let's say someone advises you to not lash out at the other person when angry. No matter how much you want to, you'll find it hard to act on this advice because spontaneity in actions is often not a conscious choice. It's a habitual reaction, a response you're wont to give. Therefore, a more pertinent question, in my view, should be: how do I change my inherent nature, so that I am able to react in a manner that befits me? So that goodness comes to me as naturally as the scent in roses? Is it even possible?

The answer is yes. It can't be done overnight though. Transformation of the subconscious is a gradual process. Steady steps with discipline are needed to accomplish this feat. Mindfulness with contemplation is the path to erase painful imprints from our subconscious, so that we don't act habitually but mindfully; so that our sudden reactions to situations and people are replaced by thoughtful responses.

The memories of our past can't be erased just by wanting to get rid of them. However, the pain associated with undesirable past experiences and memories can be allayed to a great degree by developing loving-kindness, indifference and dispassion towards memories that give us grief. Or, you could consciously meditate on erasing those psychic imprints.

Always acting in a mode of goodness does not mean that you can't be firm, push back, or protect yourself. It simply means that you can do all these without harbouring ill-will or negative feelings towards the other person. That, you can stand your ground politely by causing minimal to no grief to the other person. You will be amazed at how easy it is to be good and yet be firm by being polite.

To respond in kind or to act in a way so you teach the other person a lesson, that's easy. It's tempting even. But to hold your ground and walk the path of goodness in a sage-like manner requires a commitment to yourself. A commitment you can only keep when you are not just aware of your thoughts and emotions but are able to regulate them as well.

Mulla Nasruddin was celebrating his fiftieth marriage anniversary with great fanfare, when his friends asked him, 'What's the greatest thing you have learned in marriage, Mulla?'

'Oh I wish I could count,' he replied. 'It taught me so many things.'

'Name some.'

'Well, marriage teaches you loyalty, patience, self-restraint and forgiveness,' said Mulla. 'It teaches you how to listen, when to be quiet and so many other good qualities that you wouldn't need if you stayed single.'

Life's greatest lessons are imparted to us through difficult people. Adversities strengthen us, challenges force us to elevate ourselves. Painful experiences are almost always transformational, for they are capable of bringing out the worst or the best in us. Either way, you discover something more about yourself.

The moment you get in touch with yourself and find your spiritual footing, you will no longer have the question of how you should have acted. Thereafter, when squeezed, goodness will drip from you like honey from a hive. Like Knudsen, you'll then surprise people with your inherent goodness. Later, when they'll ask you how you could be the way you were, you will have no other response than, 'What else could I have done?'.

WHY GOOD PEOPLE SUFFER

I remember two books I enjoyed reading when I was a child. One was *Hitopodesha* and the other, *Panchtantra,* the Indian versions of *Aesop's Fables* if you will, written some two thousand years ago. I was looking for a particular story to share with you when I came across something similar in *You Don't Eat a Lion Doesn't Mean the Lion Won't Eat You* by Udaylal Pai. I've paraphrased it a bit (umm...quite a lot, actually; almost entirely, in fact):

Once upon a time, in a certain village, a young boy was walking alone by the riverside when he heard desperate cries for help.

'Please help me, save me, someone please release me,' a crocodile was shouting. He was flapping his tail, badly entangled in a net, like humans in desires.

The boy wanted to help the poor crocodile but was skeptical. 'If I help you,' he said, 'you'll eat me the moment you are free.'

The crocodile shed tears and said, 'How can I eat the person who saved my life? My kind doesn't savour their saviour. I promise that I won't even touch you and will remain eternally indebted to you.'

The boy felt pity and began to cut the net. Barely was the crocodile's head free from the net, when, as expected, it grabbed the boy's leg in its jaws, and said: 'I have been starving for a few days now...'

'What the hell!' the boy screamed. 'You damn croc, you return my goodness like this!'

'What can I do? This is the way of the world! Such is life!'

'This is so unfair!' cried the boy.

'What do you mean unfair! Ask anyone and they'll tell you that this is how the universe operates. If they prove me wrong, I'll let you go.'

The boy saw a bird perched on a nearby tree and asked, 'Do you think the crocodile's actions are fair? Is this the way of the world – full of injustice?'

The female bird had been observing the entire episode, so she quickly replied that the crocodile was right. Goodness isn't always reciprocated in kind. She, along with her partner, spent their time building a safe nest to protect their young ones, but all that mostly went to waste because the snakes would come and swallow the eggs, she apprised him. No doubt, she finished by saying, that the world was not a fair place.

'You heard it, kid,' the crocodile said, tightening its grip on the boy's slender leg. 'Let me eat you...'

'Wait…' The boy saw an old donkey that was grazing on the banks of the river and posed him the same question.

'Unfortunately, the croc is right,' the donkey said. 'I'm a donkey, everyone thinks I'm a fool and yet even I know that this world is anything but fair. Bad things happen to good people all the time. When I was young, my master loaded soiled linen on my back and extracted the maximum amount of work from me. I served him faithfully for years. Now that I am old and feeble, he has abandoned me saying that he cannot feed me. So, yes, the crocodile is right. There's great injustice, inequality and unfairness.'

'Enough now,' the crocodile said to the boy. 'I'm salivating, I can't hold it any longer. Say your prayer if you want.'

'Wait, wait,' the boy insisted. 'Just one last time, let me ask that rabbit. They say the third time's a charm.'

'Since you saved me, I'll give you one final chance.'

Upon being asked the same question, the rabbit's reply differed completely from that of the bird and the donkey.

'This is utter nonsense! It's not like that at all,' the rabbit said. 'The world is a perfectly fair place.'

'What are you talking about, you dumb bunny!' the crocodile mumbled, the boy's leg still stuck in between its jaws. 'Of course, this world is an unfair place. Look at me! I got caught in the net to begin with, for no fault of mine.'

'You sound like a man trying to talk with *paan* (betel leaf) in his mouth. I can't make sense of your mumbling, speak clearly and loudly.'

'I know where you are going with this! I'll open my mouth to speak clearly and the boy will escape.'

'You stupid or what?' said the rabbit. 'Have you forgotten how strong your tail is? If he attempts to run away, one slash and he'll be dead. You are the mightiest around here!'

The crocodile fell for this false praise and opened his mouth to continue the argument.

The rabbit screamed, 'Run boy run! Don't just stand there!' and the boy took to his heels.

The crocodile was mad with rage. 'You cheat! You took away my food. This is so unfair!'

'Look who's talking!' said the bunny, nibbling on a cherry that had dropped from the tree.

The boy rushed to the village and gathered all the menfolk. They came with their spears and swords, and killed the crocodile. His pet dog, that had come along with them, spotted the rabbit and chased it down.

'Hey! Hey!' the boy cried, trying to catch his dog. 'This rabbit saved my life. Don't attack him.' It was a bit too late though, because the dog had already buried its fangs into the rabbit's tender neck. It was no more than a lifeless ball of fur.

'Maybe the crocodile was right, after all,' the boy lamented. 'Unfairness is the way of the world! Such is life!'

After speaking to thousands of people, seeing suffering from up close, I feel it would be ignorant to still believe that there's a way out of the suffering. Here, I am not differentiating between pain (what is) and suffering (what we think it is). The Buddha proclaimed that suffering existed and that there was a way out of it. Maybe. The Vedas, too, say that if I can maintain a state of equanimity, if I can forever remember the impermanent, even unreliable, nature of this world, I won't suffer as much.

Good people suffer all the time. So much so that there's almost no direct correlation between how good or spiritual you are vis-à-vis how much suffering you may have to endure in your life. Being good or great cannot protect you from physical or mental diseases if you hit the genetic jackpot, for example. Being good doesn't mean that we can't be hit by a truck or a drunk driver. Being good has no bearing on your stock prices or the life of your loved ones. In other words, goodness grants neither immunity from nor compensation for everything that we may deem as not good.

The question that arises then is, why be good at all? If my goodness does nothing to alleviate my suffering (not directly anyway), why bother with all this goodness and kindness business? The answer is a lot more straightforward and simpler than the question itself. And that is: being good is our inherent nature. We are designed to experience happiness when we practise goodness. Therefore, people are good because it's their natural dharma. Goodness, and its cousin kindness, give us the strength to face the challenges and difficulties this life brings as regularly as the seasons.

We pray, we meditate, we act kindly, we do good because we must; that's what goodness is. It is an integral part of us. Being right is not always better than being good. We must not relinquish goodness, for it infuses strength and resilience in us. What's even more amazing is that good people can't stop being good just because the rewards are not coming through. Good people remain good. They understand that it's not a choice. Think of some of the greatest human beings. Did they retort to violence or misdemeanour just because goodness wasn't paying off?

Our challenges test us, but our attitudes shape us. Our difficulties don't break us, instead, they make us. They bring out what we have in us. Hence, good people become better, not bitter, when met with resistance.

~

The young Mulla was barely seven years old when his neighbour lured him with two dinars.

'Can you go buy two samosas from the corner shop?' he asked. 'You can eat one and bring the other one for me.'

Ten minutes later Mulla came back and said, 'Here's the balance of one dinar. The shopkeeper only had one samosa, so I had mine. Thank you.'

A good person suffers in the same way as any other. Just because someone's a good mathematician or an artist doesn't mean they can't fall sick. Rather, such a comparison is preposterous. Similarly, just because someone's spiritually evolved doesn't mean he or she is outside the purview of the laws of nature. Or in the words of Udaylal Pai: just because you don't eat a lion doesn't mean the lion won't eat you.

Does that mean we should be bad? Let me tell you, it's not in your hands. Besides, how will that help? After all, the opposite of goodness doesn't shield you from suffering either. So, what does, you'll ask? Your perspective, your attitude, your view of and your expectations from life do. When these are aligned, there may be challenges, resistance, pain, but no suffering. You may wince but you won't cry, you may crumble but you won't be crushed.

When all else fails, it's your inherent goodness alone that helps you steer the ship of life in choppy seas. Mahatma Gandhi, Nelson Mandela, Martin Luther King and many others before and after them used this basic principle to weather the ravaging storms they encountered.

It doesn't matter whether one is the boy, the crocodile, the donkey or the rabbit; there are no guarantees in life. And perhaps, this uncertainty is what makes our life adventurous.

Goodness is prayer, it is meditation. In fact, goodness is God. Be good.

BETRAYAL OF TRUST

Should we have blind faith in a Guru?

Often, I get asked questions around gurus, the role of a guru, surrendering to your guru, how much one should trust their guru and so on. A lovely reader who has been following my blog for a while, and has already read my memoir, once wrote to me. She was greatly, and perhaps rightly, distressed after reading an article about Satyananda (1923–2009), a famous yoga guru, whose ashram in Australia was under investigation for child sexual abuse. She wrote:

> *After mulling over this issue for some time, and after I read your memoir, I have some conclusions:*
>
> 1. *A guru is still human and not all of them are free from samskara. Hence the many cases of abusive gurus. A guru is in a position of absolute power and like George Orwell said, 'Power corrupts and absolute power corrupts absolutely.' A true guru, clear of bondage, does not abuse this power.*

2. ***Separate the teachings from the guru*** (emphasis mine). *Despite this issue I still think the yoga knowledge they passed on is good. So, take the good, leave the bad alone. If the guru cannot give anything good anymore – move on. Like you moved on from Baba. Like Buddha moved on from his teachers Alara and Udaka.*

I wish it was that easy – to separate the teachings from the guru. It's certainly not impossible, but it ain't a breeze either. I am not sure if I can give you a satisfactory answer, nevertheless, let me share my views on this important subject.

I've written in the past that the relationship between a guru and a disciple is like no other because it's free from the usual give and take. But an important question to be asked is who is a guru or what makes a person a guru? Wearing the robe, completing a certain course, being able to meditate, or being capable of giving a discourse, or having disciples, does not make one a guru.

Anyone can don a robe – white, black, ochre or any other, it doesn't matter. Just like people study physics or English literature, they can study Vedic or yogic literature, too; there's practically no difference – one exposes you to one school of thought, the other, to another. Anyone who isn't afraid of putting in the effort can be a meditator or an orator. Insofar as having disciples is concerned, you can find ample takers for any philosophy in this world. Even the most absurd philosophies, the dumbest teachers or preachers can garner huge followings. A large following has absolutely no connection with the worthiness of a guru. It simply means the guru appeals to the masses. For that matter, even a potato or a pumpkin has mass appeal.

Look at the most successful meditation, yoga or spiritual movements of all time, where followers have devoted their entire lives to the guru, sect or the movement. How many have actually reached a state of enlightenment though? None. (At least, I haven't met anyone who has.) Ever wondered why? Let me tell you honestly, my first guiding principle: *no one has ever gained enlightenment in an ashram, temple or a monastery.* When a guru tells you to follow his or her system for realization or heaven, they are fooling you. You deserve better. They can call it this meditation or that meditation, this *kriya* or that *kriya,* but it doesn't matter. These are merely frameworks and systems, and they work because when it comes to spirituality, a lot of people are happy with very little.

If you are going to put someone on a pedestal because they deliver a good sermon or because they are charming or knowledgeable, your chances of getting hurt go up exponentially. You may be mistaking a competent performer or a good marketer for a guru. They will turn you into puppets, they will utilize you to further their cause and they will exercise control over you just because you are letting them. And this leads me to give you my second guiding principle: *Don't accept someone as your guru just because they have bowled you over.* Follow them only if you would like to be like them.

If your guru teaches you to stay away from anger but you see him shouting, he's a hypocrite. If you sense greed and selfishness in him, if you see him telling lies while he asks you to practise the truth, he's a hypocrite. When you see that even though he preaches love and compassion, but, no matter what the cause, his ashrams are more important to him than the well-being and welfare of those who look up to him, he's a hypocrite. Please open your eyes and wake up. Abandon him. Don't accept the wrong just because your guru is doing it. And, that leads me to an extremely important point: what is wrong?

When what they say is not what they do, it's wrong. For example, if Osho slept with a woman, I wouldn't call it wrong because he never said he didn't. If Ramdev did, however, I would flag it as misconduct because he says he's a celibate. So long as their actions match their words, I don't see a betrayal. When your guru is open and honest, they are not wrong, even if you disagree with them. At that time, you have the choice to stay or go. And, by open and honest, I don't mean they have to hand you their personal diary (unless they ask you for yours). If their actions or conduct don't sit well with you, move on. Because not everything needs to be judged, and just like you, your guru, too, is entitled to have a life of his own.

Having said that, I can tell you what *is* wrong regardless of how liberal your guru may be or how spiritual the situation may seem. When people are hurt, abused, molested, or mistreated, it's always wrong. Always. When you are asked to lie to fellow followers for any cause whatsoever, it's always wrong. When your guru tells you his way is the only way, it's the biggest lie. When you see wrong, don't put up with it and don't just leave. Speak up. Learn to trust your inner voice. Not all gurus are bad though. Even in this day and age where many of them are crooks, there are plenty of honest and good gurus, too. If you walk the path sincerely, Nature will arrange for a guru in your life. Take my word for it.

Before you accept someone as your guru, take your time. Examine him or her thoroughly. Repeatedly. Pointedly. Take them as your guru only when you absolutely accept what they represent and want to become like them. Once you are ready, put your trust not in your guru but in what they stand for. Because, when you place your trust in a phenomenon and not just a person, when you invest your sentiments in a belief or a cause and not just its proponent, it no longer remains just trust, it becomes faith. And, faith, unlike trust, can never be betrayed because true faith is unconditional. It's not based on anything.

Guru is not a position of absolute power but a conduit of unreasonable compassion. He will never abuse power because he doesn't hold any power to begin with; only love. A true guru will never tell you to tread his path blindly, instead he'll encourage you to find your own. He's gentle like the flowing river, warm like the winter sun, bright like the full moon, rejuvenating like the first summer rain. And, if you don't feel gentle, warm, bright and rejuvenated yourself in his company, he's not the right guru for you.

YOUR OPINION ABOUT YOURSELF

Once upon a time, a thief hadn't had any luck for many days in a row. One night, he went out resolved he wouldn't return home empty-handed. He scoured the streets looking for the right home, the right opportunity, but in vain. Tired and dejected, in the wee hours of the morning, he fell asleep on a footpath.

A few minutes later, a drunkard was passing by. He saw the thief and felt sorry for him thinking he was also some drunk who had passed out on the street. He stopped by to see if there was any bottle lying nearby because that's what he was interested in – more liquor. But, there was none. Angry, he left. Hardly had he gone when another man, who happened to be a gambler, saw the sleeping thief.

'Poor loser,' he thought. 'He must have lost so much that he's scared to go home.'

An hour passed and another thief happened to pass this way. He looked at the sleeping man and thought, 'He must be an unfortunate small-time burglar like me who couldn't get his hands on anything tonight.'

Dawn was breaking over the horizon when a yogi was going to a nearby river for his ablutions. He looked at the thief and began admiring him.

'This is a real yogi,' he thought. 'Unlike me, who's still caught up in rituals, he's just lying here carefree, without any belongings. This is the way of a yogi.'

He derived deep inspiration from the thief, bowed before him and moved on.

Another hour passed. The sun, now warm and bright, woke the thief, who left for his home, empty-handed.

This is how our world operates. It doesn't matter who, how or what you are (or aren't), each one will regard you according to their individual capacity. They will form their opinion based on their own perceptions and preconceived notions about you. Some will think you are a thief while others will label you a gambler. Some may mistake you for a drunk and some may see you as a yogi. Often, most of what they think about you is dependent on them, their own conditioning. It is not as much about you as it is about them. The more you realize this, the less bothered you will be by their opinions.

I once read a quote: 'You'll worry less about what people think about you when you realize how seldom they do.' And, even when people do think about you, often it is more along the lines of what they want to think about you. As they grow and evolve, as their priorities change, they begin to think differently. They may or may not admit that their opinions about you have changed, because our world expects consistency in everything. A change in opinion is not always taken so kindly. But regardless of whether they express it or not, as their own consciousness expands, they'll see you in a new light. There is, therefore, little wisdom in chasing ever-elusive thoughts of others.

I am not suggesting that you should lead a debauched life completely disregarding others, thinking that, well, their opinions about you are wrong, but, I'm stating that, sooner rather than later, it is a question you must ask yourself: to what extent are you willing to stretch yourself to gain others' positive opinion of you? How important is it to you that others think highly of you? Quite interestingly, though not surprisingly, almost all of us want to be in the good books of others. We want others to think highly of us. There's a certain sense of fulfilment and accomplishment, when others approve of your own opinion about yourself.

The funny thing is they, too, are working hard, so you may see them and think of them in a certain way. Both want to create an impact on the other person to ultimately accomplish the same outcome: feel good about oneself. This urge to seek others' approval is one of the strongest urges one has; it's almost innate. Because since childhood, we are constantly seeking the approval of others. Someone else is always marking us against a criteria they've set. We are always matching it. In doing so, we are eternally manipulating ourselves. This leads to great inner unrest and turmoil. One of the definitive ways to rise above others' opinions is to turn inward. And, how exactly to turn inward, you may wonder.

If you are honest with yourself, if you are leading a meaningful life, if you take a pause and reflect on your life and your actions, you'll automatically begin to turn inward. Countless virtues will bloom in your heart like flowers do in spring. An inward mind leads to contentment. What others have to say about you will bother you less and less then. Turning inward doesn't mean that we become so selfish that we are only focused on ourselves. On the contrary, it means seeing ourselves as an extension of the universe. It is feeling the interconnectedness in everything there is. And, with this experiential understanding dawns the wisdom that you are complete, that you are a universe in your own right. And that, in *your* universe there's plenty of space for everyone and their views.

If, based on your actions, you see yourself a certain way and believe that with utmost conviction, the world will start seeing you that way too (if at all that matters to you). Because, everything is interconnected and interdependent. Absolutely everything. Whether you choose to be the sun, a moon, or just any star in your own galaxy, it's your personal choice. The greater your magnitude, the less affected you are by the smaller stars.

How you see yourself matters a great deal more than how others see you because your happiness and peace is dependent on your own honest view about yourself.

And, by the way, in the end, it doesn't matter whether one is seen as a thief or a yogi. In the end, both will go empty-handed. Everyone does.

HONOURING YOUR WORD

What's more important to follow: your head or your heart?

'Lieutenant,' the Major warned, 'you are not going back there.'

'I am sorry, sir,' replied the lieutenant. 'I must.'

'You are disobeying my orders. Plus, he must be dead by now.'

'I am sorry, sir, but I must go back to save my friend.'

Legend has it that it happened for real. In the Vietnam war, a company of US soldiers ended up in an enemy area and were under heavy fire. Everyone in the group managed to escape unharmed except one soldier who was fatally wounded. John, a lieutenant, insisted on going back and rescuing his friend. The Major forbade him from doing so, but John was unrelenting.

'You know the code,' the Major yelled. 'I order you not to go back unless this be your last day in the army.'

'You can fire me, Major. But, I must go back.'

'You will live to regret it, Lieutenant.'

Without saying another word, violating protocol and ignoring his superior's orders, the young lieutenant rushed back to the besieged region. He elbowed his way to his friend, who was gasping for breath. They exchanged a few words that were barely audible under the sound of constant bombing and firing. Against all odds, John took his friend on his back like a rucksack and carefully trod the difficult terrain. By the time they got back to the camp though, his friend had already breathed his last.

'What did I tell ya?' the major shouted. 'Was it worth risking your life to save a dead man?'

'Sir, he's not a dead man but a martyr,' the lieutenant replied softly. 'I'm mighty glad I went back because my dying friend and fellow-soldier gripped my hand tightly and kept saying just one thing.'

There was a short silence and even the major went soft for a moment.

'Sir,' the lieutenant continued, 'he said, "I knew you would come back for me." That's all he said, sir. And, it was worth more than everything put together.'

Most of us hold our life and relationships together on the basis of promises we make or those that are made to us. Promise is perhaps a synonym for hope, for the hopes our loved ones keep based on words we give. Making a commitment is the easy part, whether that's a new year resolution or reading your marital vows at the sacred altar. What is hard is to honour them. But, honour we must. For every time we keep our word, we grow a bit more. It not only gives a tremendous boost to our willpower, it also makes us more spiritual.

No doubt that honouring a word can drain you out. That is the case particularly when an inner battle is going on, where your mind wants to do one thing but your heart is set on quite another, when emotions defeat reason. Having said that, even an hour at the gym or cooking a meal in the kitchen can be exhausting and yet if we want good health and fresh food, we do what we ought to do. Keeping a word is no different; it may not be joyous or desirable, but in the end, it leaves us with a sublime sense of pride and fulfilment. To be able to put your hand on your heart and say, 'I did the best I could; I lived by my promise,' not only boosts your self-esteem and morale, it also prepares you to take on the bigger challenges of life with a certain effortlessness.

Besides, there's a good spiritual reason for honouring our word: we get closer to the divinity within us. Any promise we make is not necessarily a pact between us and others but it is between us and the Divine (call it God, Universe or anything else you wish). For, in the final analysis it's not between us and them. Instead, it's between us and us alone. And, at all times, we should act in a manner that befits us.

~

Mulla Nasruddin's dying father was determined to take his wealth with him to the other world.

Handing him a bag containing $100,000 in cash, he said to the Imam, 'Promise me, that you will put this money in the coffin with my dead body.'

He gave two other bags with $100,000 each to his doctor and Mulla, on the same condition. Each one of them promised him that they would do the needful. Six months after his death, they got together and the inevitable subject came up.

'I am somewhat ashamed to say this,' the Imam confessed, 'but I needed money for restoration of the mosque, so I only put $60,000 in the casket.'

'You are still better than me,' said the doctor. 'I took out $75,000 for my own needs and kept only $25,000 back in the coffer.'

'What about you, Mulla?' they asked him, since he had sat through their disclosures with a disgusted look on his face.

'What do you think?' Mulla spoke, as if chiding them. 'I kept my promise and put the entire sum in the coffin.'

'The whole $100,000?' the other two exclaimed.

'You bet!' said Mulla. 'In fact, saving him the hassle of lugging around all that money, I wrote him a check. He can cash it whenever he likes.'

At times, like Mulla's father, we ask for absurd promises that don't benefit anyone in any way other than giving us a false sense of comfort. At other times, like Mulla, we find loopholes in our truth to suit ourselves. Either way, it weakens us spiritually. The easiest way to keep your promises is to first be mindful of the words you utter and then take them one day at a time. *All I've got to do is keep my promise today, this hour, this minute. I just have to honour them from one moment to another, from one inhalation to the next.* When we live with such awareness, we can gracefully survive an entire lifetime with our vows intact. This is the secret of spiritual strength and attainment.

What if we kept our promises like Nature keeps its promises? A natural order will automatically manifest in our lives. Granted that on rare occasions, Nature falters too (like an unexpected downpour or a heat wave in winter, etc.). But most times, it honours its seasons. If each one of us made a sincere effort to come through on our words, our world would become increasingly beautiful and forgiving. To falter is only human, to forgive divine. To falter again is irresponsible. And to forgive again ... could be either co-dependency or supreme compassion.

Amidst all the distractions and temptations, we have a duty to speak and act with sincerity. To keep a word of honour is to build a world of honour.

IV
AWAKENING

THE SPIRIT OF SERVICE

Do heaven and hell really exist?

Legend has it that the valiant ruler of Mewar, Maharana Pratap, was once sitting with a humble attendant of his. The year was 1580, when he had been overpowered in an ongoing conflict with the Mughals. Although five years later, Maharana would reclaim most of his empire, presently, however, he was keeping a low profile, pouring all his energies into rebuilding his army. During these uncertain times, when he was living frugally, he was sent two mangoes by one of his subjects.

His servant cut the mangoes into eight parts and arranged them on a plate. They looked ripe, luscious and inviting.

'Tell me how it tastes,' said Maharana Pratap, giving the first piece to the servant.

'Hukum,' the servant replied, pausing to relish the mango a bit and then continued, 'it is most delicious!' And he requested another piece.

A bit surprised, Maharana handed him one more, and this piece, too, the servant gobbled down in a flash, pleading for more. The king was taken aback at this unusual behaviour but out of care for a man who had been serving him for ages, he obliged.

'Please,' the Maharana's servant begged, 'I'm starving. Give me the rest and I'll personally go and fetch new mangoes for you.'

In practically no time, he ate all the seven pieces one after another, while the king's expression changed from that of amusement and compassion to disbelief and disgust.

'You thankless rascal!' Maharana thundered. 'You are unfit to serve me.' And with that, he put the last piece of the mango in his mouth, only to spit it out the next moment.

'You call this sour and bitter mango delicious?' he exclaimed. 'It tastes horrible!'

'I seek your forgiveness,' the servant said. 'For years, you have fed me and my family. You have protected us through thick and thin. I can't give you anything in return, but at least, I could make sure you didn't have to taste those sour mangoes.'

It is fair to expect love in return of love. It is normal to desire acknowledgement of our efforts or recognition of our talents and work. Friendships and relationships thrive when people reciprocate in kind. The spirit of service, however, is an entirely different matter. Service expects nothing in return except the well-being of the one we are serving.

True service requires absolute selflessness, something even beyond altruism, for in service, the benchmark is not set on whether you are acknowledged or special. Instead, your goal is to devote everything you've got to serve the cause that matters to you. And there lies the paradox, the more we devote ourselves wholeheartedly to our mission, without worrying about recognition, the greater the success and satisfaction we derive from walking the path.

Sometimes, people ask me what is surrender and how we surrender to a cause/person? Service is surrender. Without surrender, true service is not possible and without service, surrender dies a quick death. Surrender is that feeling at heart that makes us let go. It helps us be at ease and relax. It makes us understand that we don't have to control everything that is going on in our lives. In fact, we can't. Service, then, is devoting ourselves wholeheartedly to what we do control: our response, actions, and words to whatever comes our way.

In the *Hasidic Masters' Guide to Management,*[17] Moshe Kranc cites a beautiful parable (variations of which are found in every culture):

> I once ascended to the firmaments. I first went to see Hell and the sight was horrifying. Row after row of tables were laden with platters of sumptuous food, yet the people seated around the tables were pale and emaciated, moaning in hunger. As I came closer, I understood their predicament.

Every person held a full spoon, but both arms were splinted with wooden slats so he could not bend either elbow to bring the food to his mouth. It broke my heart to hear the tortured groans of these poor people as they held their food so near but could not consume it.

Next I went to visit Heaven. I was surprised to see the same setting I had witnessed in Hell – row after row of long tables laden with food. But in contrast to Hell, the people here in Heaven were sitting contentedly talking with each other, obviously sated from their sumptuous meal.

As I came closer, I was amazed to discover that here, too, each person had his arms splinted on wooden slats that prevented him from bending his elbows. How, then, did they manage to eat?

As I watched, a man picked up his spoon and dug it into the dish before him. Then he stretched across the table and fed the person across from him! The recipient of this kindness thanked him and returned the favor by leaning across the table to feed his benefactor.

I suddenly understood. Heaven and Hell offer the same circumstances and conditions. The critical difference is in the way the people treat each other.

I ran back to Hell to share this solution with the poor souls trapped there. I whispered in the ear of one starving man, 'You do not have to go hungry. Use your spoon to feed your neighbor, and he will surely return the favor and feed you.'

> 'You expect me to feed the detestable man sitting across the table?' said the man angrily. 'I would rather starve than give him the pleasure of eating!'

When our attention shifts from worrying about ourselves to adding value to the lives of those around us and serving a greater cause, our inherent goodness rises to the surface. All becomes possible then. Good things become great in due course. Good people become great people with the passage of time. This is the natural progression. For goodness does not focus on making a name but making a difference. And that's what service does: it makes a difference.

The ability to care for and serve others is what distinguishes an ordinary person from an enlightened one.

AWAKENING

Does enlightenment mean you will forever surf the waves of bliss?

'How do I gain enlightenment?' someone said to me one day. 'Can you not grant me some deep experience? I want a radical change in my life.'

I get this asked frequently by many enthusiastic seekers. They are in search of a panacea, some mystical reality that will solve all their problems (spiritual and emotional) forever. While many aspirants understand the importance of persistence and individual effort, most others are looking for a quick fix. Here's a beautiful quote by Adyashanti[18] that mirrors my own thoughts in more ways than one:

> Many seekers do not take full responsibility for their own liberation, but wait for one big, final spiritual experience which will catapult them fully into it. It is this search for the final liberating experience which gives rise to a rampant form of

> spiritual consumerism in which seekers go from one teacher to another, shopping for enlightenment as if shopping for sweets in a candy store. This spiritual promiscuity is rapidly turning the search for enlightenment into a cult of experience for seekers. And, while many people indeed have powerful experiences, in most cases these do not lead to the profound transformation of the individual, which is the expression of enlightenment.

One of the greatest misconceptions about enlightenment is that it will just happen. That's not the case. It has to be earned, it has to be lived. Sometimes, I find it challenging to explain to seekers that true enlightenment is not a one-off special moment, but more a culmination of lifelong experiences and practices that result in the dawning of a great insight. I don't blame them for thinking that by the magical touch of some guru or maybe by being struck by lightning, they will arrive at a moment of enlightenment. Partly because we have plenty of spiritual books out there that give that impression. Even I may have inadvertently conveyed the same by sharing one of my most defining spiritual experiences in my memoir. For that matter, the Buddha's enlightenment under the Bodhi tree is often construed as an isolated event of extraordinary significance. It was anything but that.

In comprehending and highlighting such experiences, we tend to overlook the tremendous amount of effort that goes in realizing that state. For a moment, think of enlightenment as winning the Nobel Prize. We can't have it just by visiting other Nobel laureates and we certainly can't be awarded it just because we want it. After a lifetime of commitment to a cause or producing a phenomenal body of work, and assuming the circumstances are favourable, the committee might consider your nomination and grant you one. No doubt winning the Nobel Prize will bring about a change in your life and lifestyle to a degree, you will inspire more people and so on. But, beyond that, there's not much. It's not going to improve your relationships, it's not going to, for instance, fix your physical health. Those challenges will remain.

Without preparation and readiness, any spiritual experience is hardly transformational. And if an experience doesn't trigger some kind of lasting transformation in you, however subtle, it holds little meaning ultimately. When you continue to walk the path sincerely, diligently, many learnings, lessons and experiences give you the wisdom to lead your life differently. Differently so in a manner that it's more conducive to retaining a state of bliss. Having said that, even if you are enlightened, it doesn't mean that you won't experience pain or that you will always find joy in everything that goes on in your life.

R.K. Laxman (1921–2015), one of India's most famous cartoonists ever, writes a lovely passage in *The Distorted Mirror*.[19]

> People are curious about my profession and try to clear their doubts by putting all sorts of questions.

Recently a lady asked me, 'Do you do the drawings for your cartoons yourself?' I answered, 'Yes, I do.' Then she questioned, 'And the captions to the cartoons, do you write them too?' 'Of course,' I said. And, finally, she asked, 'The ideas for the cartoons, don't say you think them up too?'

...

There is one [question] that is rather rarely asked but which makes me go into deep introspection. This is: 'When you look around, does everything appear funny to you?'

A cartoonist does not lead a charmed life of perpetual fun out of the reach of the cares and worries that bedevil his fellow men. The fluctuating prices of onions affect me in the same way as they delight or outrage a primary schoolteacher. Likewise, taxes depress my spirit. Bores at the mike, and traffic jams drive me crazy. Surely a doctor does not always look at life in terms of coughs, colds, allergies and bronchial inflammations. A star of the silver screen, I am sure, has enough sense to know that beyond the range of the camera life does not continue to be full of idyllic scenes, sex, songs and ketchup-blood. Why, then, should a cartoonist see living caricatures and hear rib-tickling dialogue all around him? So I comfort myself with the self-assurance that my view of life is normally as banal as that of the next man in the queue for sugar or kerosene.

Enlightenment is something like that. It does not mean that you don't feel the pain or remain eternally unaffected by everything that goes around you. All of that we must go through based on our karma, temperament and attitude towards life. The only thing that changes is that you grow into a more spiritual being, you become increasingly resilient and kind. What life hurls at you doesn't change. How you catch it or dodge it, does. When it builds to a tipping point, you become kind of independent, very independent. Less worried about what the world thinks of you, how it perceives you and so on. In other words, you draw your own cartoons, write your own captions and, much to the fascination or disbelief of others, come up with the ideas, too.

As the famous Zen saying goes, 'Before enlightenment: chop wood, fetch water. After enlightenment: chop wood, fetch water.'

Being a *jivan-mukta,* a liberated soul, or an enlightened person does not relieve one of his/her duties. Self-realization is not, as Eknath Easwaran put it, a compensation for one's good deeds. It is but simply an outlook towards life that you gain from experiential understanding. If you really wish to get a grip on the notion of enlightenment, look upon it as a way of life, a commitment to virtues, as a promise to carry yourself a certain way and leading your life in a manner that befits you.

Liberation is not plonking a glorious flag on top of Mount Everest, it is but a mindful and diligent journey meandering through many treks and hikes, stopping and camping along the way, meeting and greeting fellow travellers, absorbing the breathtaking views, appreciating the challenges, rejoicing in where you are already. All this, while you remain inward-focused but goal-oriented.

When you realize this, a better sense of well-being and happiness shrouds you. You understand that there are no dark moments, that you are already enlightened. You just need to live a certain way to experience it. Then you laugh at the discovery of how seriously, unnecessarily so, you've been taking yourself. As Thich Naht Hanh said:

> I laugh when I think how I once sought paradise as a realm outside of the world of birth. It is right in the world of birth and death that the miraculous truth is revealed. But this is not the laughter of someone who suddenly acquires a great fortune; neither is it the laughter of one who has won a victory. It is, rather, the laughter of one who, after having painfully searched for something for a long time, finds it one morning in the pocket of his coat.[20]

~

A religious man invited a monk to come bless his new home. The monk politely turned down the request saying he's busy.

'But, what are you doing?' the man insisted.

'Nothing.'

Thinking that the monk was perhaps not in a mood to visit that day, he let it be and phoned again the next day. 'Can you come today to bless my home?'

'Sorry,' said the monk, 'I'm busy.'

'Doing what?'

'I'm doing nothing,' replied the monk.

'But that was what you were doing yesterday!' said the man.

'Right,' the monk replied. 'I'm not finished yet!'

Enlightenment, too, is an ongoing affair. No doubt, there can be a transformational moment that changes something in you forever. Living that change, however, is a matter of mindfulness and more. True enlightenment, that.

This is it. This life. It's beautiful. Live it. Love it. For yourself, for others. Laugh it away. That's all there is to know. Most of the rest, life can do without.

THE SECRET OF BEING POSITIVE

Can being positive help us lead more fulfilled lives?

How to be positive? I get asked this question a lot. And often when people say they want to be positive, what they are really saying is they want to be happy and hopeful under almost all circumstances. That, I don't want to feel frustrated and agitated in the face of adversity, that somehow I want to be at peace.

The truth is that life is hard work and there's no one easy way to be positive all the time. Having said that, we can learn to be mostly positive. Even those who appear naturally positive and confident learned to be that way, consciously or otherwise. Before I impart my two cents' worth on positivity, allow me to share a little something with you.

Shuffled through many foster homes, Jarvis Jay Masters had a rather difficult childhood. Violence became his answer to protect himself, his coping mechanism. At nineteen, he ended up in prison on a ten-year sentence and later, charged with the murder of a prison guard (while Jarvis was locked in his cell at the time of the incident!), he was handed a death sentence. From death row, in his book, *Finding Freedom*,[21] he writes an interesting observation. Here it is, slightly paraphrased:

'Check out Channel Seven, Jarvis,' my neighbour said from his next cell one evening, while I was reading a book on meditation. 'They're showing a Ku Klux Klan rally in Louisiana. Klansmen screaming and shouting all that supremacy garbage. Did you hear what they were saying?'

'Nah, man. I missed it. I have the volume turned down,' I said, glancing up at the TV. 'I did see a bunch of angry faces and racist posters, though.'

About ten minutes later, Omar hollered, 'Hey, Jarvis! Man, check out all those people. It must be a thousand folks marching in San Francisco. Do you see them?'

'Wow!' I said, looking up at the huge demonstration on my screen. 'What's up with them?'

'The environmentalists are demanding an end to the cutting of trees in some places. They are saying the planet is being destroyed, and more and more wildlife species are near extinction.'

'Is that right? I can tell just by looking that they're upset. You see that one woman raging into the microphone and those demonstrators holding up posters and shouting and getting arrested? They all must be pretty pissed to be screaming like that.'

A little later, Omar yelled, 'Hey, check that out. Still watching? Look at the president and all those congressmen, right there on national TV, fighting and arguing, each trying to convince the public that the other is at fault for this terrible economy.'

'Yeah, I see them. Is that what they're fussing about? I can tell they're in an uproar about something. That one senator, man, he's almost spitting. But you know what's really interesting, Omar?'

'No, what's that?'

'The anger and bitterness on the faces of these congressmen and the president of the USA is the same as on the faces of all those environmentalists and the Klansmen. They are just a bunch of angry people.'

Anger, rage, negativity are common, if not natural, human emotions. Majority of the people experience them on a daily basis, many times a day. At home, at work, in a supermarket, on a train, everywhere we have people around us. Most of these people are going through a lot in their lives. Some of them will take out their anger on themselves, some will direct it on governments, on their loved ones, some on you and so on. A bunch of angry people. Do you want to be like them?

That's how this world can be. Angry and ruthless. Now what do we do? We have a choice. We can either be angry ourselves and become like them or we can make a conscious choice about what we want to think, speak and how we want to act. To experience peace in the world, you must be at peace within. And the more you are at peace within, the more centred you will be.

A centred person may not experience bouts of happiness if you see what I mean. He or she may not have tidal waves of enthusiasm, but they will have a sustainable flow of realistic positivity, like the gentle flow of a river in winter. The more truthful and real you are in your thoughts, speech and conduct, the more positive and happy you'll be.

Simplicity is the seed of inner peace.

~

One evening, Grandma sent her grandson Johnny down to the water hole to fetch some water for cooking dinner. As he was dipping the bucket in, he saw two big eyes looking back at him. Dropping the bucket, he ran back to the kitchen.

'Where's the water?' she asked him. 'And my bucket?'

'I can't get any water from that water hole, Grandma,' Johnny exclaimed. 'There's a big old alligator down there!'

'Now don't you mind that alligator, Johnny. He's been there for years and he's never hurt anyone. He's probably as scared of you as you are of him!'

'Well, Grandma,' replied Johnny, 'if he's as scared of me as I am of him then that water ain't fit to drink!'

If the storm of anger and hatred in our inner world is raging as badly as the one outside, then this world will become unfit for living. Diseases of the mind and body manifest much quicker in the one who possesses an irate mind, a resentful consciousness. A simple heart, a content soul on the other hand is naturally at peace, and, therefore, positive.

As non-monastic Buddhist Layman Pang (740–808) said, 'When the mind is at peace, the world too is at peace. Nothing real, nothing absent. Not holding on to reality, not getting stuck in the void, you are neither holy nor wise, just an ordinary fellow who has completed his work.'

I suppose that's what I mean by simplicity. That, we are humble, real, centred, and honest about ourselves. Hope, positivity and happiness are the birds that live in the nest of contentment. You will face difficult people, situations and circumstances. Adversities will greet you every step of the way. Such is life. Now what? Are you going to give up, give in, or keep walking one step at a time? That simple and honest discipline of not giving up will grant you peace and positivity.

Being positive isn't always the same as being happy though. Sometimes, all it means is that you are at peace, you are at ease.

Being positive comes naturally to the one who leads a life sans pretense. If you are honest about yourself, you will be realistic about what you can or can't do. Such realism will help you in being positive. This is the secret of positivity.

Be real, be simple.

FROM SUFFERING TO HAPPINESS

How can we find that elusive happiness?

Sometimes (very often, in fact), I meet those who are single. Generally, they are looking for the right person, a companion to spend their life with. They have been either hurt in the past or just haven't found the perfect match yet. No one's waiting for them when they get to their empty home in the evening. They wake up by themselves, with no one next to them. Loneliness and the probability of growing old alone haunt them every now and then. All they want is to love and to be loved but they can't find anyone to whom they can say these things; they tell me.

And then, I meet those who are married. While they love their family, they long for a period of peace and rest. They feel tied down by their commitments. They have come to understand that marriage is a synonym of compromise and requires tremendous sacrifice on a daily basis, at all levels. There are changes they want to see around the house, in their partner, kids and so on, before they think they can be truly happy. All they wanted was to love and be loved; they'd even married someone who they thought fit the bill. But it now feels like they married the wrong person, they say.

In their quest for true love, either way, as far as I'm concerned, the outcome of every meeting is the same. Almost every time. In two parts:

1. I see my box of tissues depleting faster than the water level in Delhi's municipal tank.
2. I hear the same questions. Why? Why me? Why doesn't he/she realize? Why am I suffering? How can God do this to me?

The tissue issue is easy. I just put a new box to manage the tear ducts. We can wipe the tears we shed. The second one, however, is a bit more complicated. Let me share with you a short story before I offer my perspective.

The Mughal emperor Akbar once asked his courtiers who, between God and Akbar, was more powerful. The ministers were in a fix because, clearly, the answer was God, but to say that anyone was greater than the king might mean getting your next haircut with a guillotine. And giving the wrong answer, which would be perceived as blatant flattery, might still result in the same fate. One by one though, deciding to speak the truth, everyone said that God was more potent than their emperor. Everyone but one person.

The wisest man in the royal court, Birbal, proclaimed that Akbar was indeed more powerful than God. The courtiers secretly rejoiced seeing Birbal in a soup. Finally, it was out in the open that he was sucking up to the king, they thought.

'Obviously, you just want to impress me, Birbal,' the king spoke sternly, shaking his head. 'I'm disgusted at your blasphemous reply. How can I be more powerful than God?'

'His Excellency,' replied Birbal, 'indeed, our emperor is more powerful than God. God is beyond discrimination and favouritism. He is bound by dharma. Every act of God is in line with the meticulous working of the infinite Universe. But, your highness is not bound by any law. You can punish anyone even if he is innocent. God can't do that.'

Praising Birbal, Akbar rewarded him amply. Later in the evening, when Birbal's wife heard what had transpired in the court, she confronted him gently, asking him not to give such risky answers in the future. And why would he even do that?

'Because,' Birbal replied calmly, 'it was an ignorant question.'

I agree with Birbal wholeheartedly. You really think that someone up there is giving you the stick or the lollies based on how cleverly you call out to him? I doubt it.

God cannot solve our relationship problems because He did not create them in the first place. It has nothing to do with God, Universe or Nature. We suffer when we are unable to handle ourselves, our emotions and our circumstances.

Don't get me wrong, I believe in the existence of God. The whole existence is God for that matter. I see God as the endless compassion, beauty and bliss that flow through our infinite Universe. But I don't think that being a love-guru, matchmaker or magistrate is part of His job description. Nature runs its course most indiscriminately and dispassionately, with the greatest detachment.

~

A man went to a tailor to collect his suit he'd given for stitching a week earlier.

'Sorry, sir,' the tailor said, 'it's not done yet. God willing, it'll be ready in three days.'

The disappointed customer came back three days later, but got the same reply: 'God willing, sir, I'll definitely finish it in a week's time.'

The customer shouted at the tailor and went away disgruntled. Much to his chagrin, a week later, the tailor still hadn't sewn the suit.

'God willing, sir,' he pleaded, 'it should be ready in four days.'

'Listen up, buddy,' the customer said, 'let's keep God out of this. Tell me how long it will take if God is not willing.'

Imagine there was no help available from any external source. How would you have gone about finding your happiness? For, to be honest with you, I don't think Grace means that our lives' problems will end. I don't believe that we pray or are religious, so we may talk some God into our traps of desires.

If happiness is what you seek, begin with the premise that no one else can give it to you. Anyone who wants someone else to make them feel fulfilled, often ends up being only more discontent. As Goethe once said, 'From the power that binds all beings, that man frees himself who overcomes himself.'

The only way to end our suffering is to overcome ourselves. Other people in our lives are merely enablers and catalysts of the suffering we already carry within us. Suffering is another name for our inability to come to terms with life. When it comes to inner peace, the greater our acceptance and understanding of our circumstances and the people around us, the more peaceful we are.

The path to bliss and peace begins with responsibility. Take responsible steps, speak responsible words, act responsibly. Before long, you will find the joy of inner peace straining against your consciousness, like the spring breeze against the blooming trees, caressing your soul, filling your cup. From the noise of expectations, like the rustle of cicadas on a midsummer day stridulating passionately from the dry grass of desires, your whole being will murmur with bliss, like the gentle mountain stream under the soft winter sun.

Be responsible. Be gentle. Be happy.

A STORY OF GRACE

Can divine grace truly protect us from adversities?

The tale you are about to read belongs to Swami Raghvananda, the erstwhile Pradeep Brahmachari, who took care of me when I meditated in the Himalayan woods. Raghu Swami, for that's what I call him, is also one of the most devoted disciples I've ever known, full of life and detachment. This story is about faith and grace, of simplicity and morality.

Nearly thirty-three years ago when Raghu Swami was barely seven years old, his father had not received his salary for nearly six months. He had been transferred to a far-off location, but accepting the transfer would have meant welcoming several disadvantages. Firstly, if he joined the new place, he wouldn't have been transferred back for a long time. Reporting at the new venue would have also meant renting a house (and he already owned one, the house where he stayed at the time) and changing kids' schools, moving everything, among other tasks.

It would not have been financially viable given the meagre government salary he earned. So, everyone advised him not to accept the transfer order and instead, apply for cancelling it. He followed the advice.

Six months, however, is a long time and the family ran out of whatever savings they had had. The electricity was disconnected within the first three months due to non-payment of the bill. There was no money to buy candles or oil for the lamps. So much so, there came a day when there was absolutely nothing left in the kitchen to cook or eat. Not even rice or salt. The family of five had no clue how they would get their food the next day, let alone that evening. The corrupt government officials extended no help and continually asked for more money to escalate his request. Raghu Swami's father had already mortgaged his wife's gold earrings and chain (the only jewellery she had other than her *mangalsutra* and a nose pin).

Looking at the empty vessels in the kitchen and no nest egg to tap into, Raghu Swami's father contemplated joining at the new location after all, but even there, he wouldn't get his salary for at least another month. Only a miracle could have put food on the table that evening.

It was on this day, a Sunday, that they were invited to a *Ramcharitmanas paath* (a religious function where disciples sing the glories of Lord Rama). Raghu Swami's elder sister was too shy to go, she said. Especially, since the parents weren't going. And they had chosen to stay back because there was absolutely nothing to offer in the *pooja thali* (a plate containing small monetary or other gifts, which is offered to the orator). Finally, seven-year-old

Raghu Swami and his thirteen-year-old brother decided to go because Raghu Swami had been devoted to Lord Rama ever since he could recall. Besides, there would also be a yummy feast served there.

On the way to the function, when the two were walking casually, though eagerly, a man on a scooter zipped past them. A short distance away, they saw something falling out from his side pocket. Raghu Swami and his brother dashed towards the man, but he had already moved far ahead. Their eyes nearly popped out when they saw what lay on the road. It was a neat sum of money with a red rubber band around it. Having turned into one of the streets, the man on the scooter had already gone out of sight. The brothers still ran to the corner of the street, but they had lost the driver.

Not to be late for the feast, they pocketed the little bundle and rushed to the function. They were served salad, rice, lentils, potato curry, pumpkin sabzi, puris, pickle, yogurt, rice pudding and halwa. After eating to their hearts' content, the boys went on to the rooftop (where there was no one around) and counted the money. A total of 1500 rupees!

Thereafter, they galloped down to the nearest grocery store and bought 700 kg of rice and ten packets of salt with that money. They carried their groceries home on a small cart. If nothing else, Raghu Swami told me, at least they could boil rice with salt and eat that for a good few months. Everyone at home rejoiced as if they had won a jackpot. Raghu Swami's mother cried tears of gratitude. No one would sleep hungry that night.

One week later, Raghu Swami and his ten-year-old sister bunked school and went to the Chief Medical Officer (CMO) – the man responsible for granting their father's plea. They waited outside his office and insisted that they wouldn't leave without seeing him. A kind clerk let them in. They cried before the officer and narrated the whole story. Immediately, the CMO asked for the file and approved the request by cancelling the transfer. He also ordered that salary worth the six-month period, over which their father had not been paid, be released within the next two hours.

His father joined the very next day and came back home with the six months' salary that had been pending thus far. Before stocking the kitchen or taking back the pledged jewellery or paying the electricity bill, so that power could be restored, he put the entire sum at the altar and prayed. Then he called Raghu Swami and gave him 1500 rupees.

'Go and put this in any temple donation box,' he said, teary-eyed. 'God helped us when we needed his help, now we must return it.'

Every time I recall this story, I'm always overwhelmed. Who says that faith doesn't help? Grace may take time but it most certainly comes. Our world may have terrible people who harm and hurt others but it also has some beautiful people who are always eager to help others. Nature does not disappoint the one who is truthful, patient and faithful. The entire Universe conspires to pave the way for such a person. It connects you with the right person at the right time.

The most beautiful part of the story is Raghu Swami's father returning the money. This is truth and morality of the highest form, because this is sheer honesty. For the record, here's the definition of *honest* according to the Oxford English Dictionary: free of deceit; truthful and sincere.

The one who leads a life of honesty is never outside the orbit of grace. Things may not always fall in place for that person, but they won't fall apart either. If your intentions, words and actions are honest, you will radiate a divine glow, I promise. Your very glance will bestow peace upon others.

At any rate, rather than burning your heart with jealousy, envy and covetousness, it's far more rewarding to ignite the fire of truth and compassion. It burns all afflictions.

The lamp of bliss lights most gloriously in the heart of an honest person.

THE COURSE OF GRIEF

Why are we unable to get over grief?

It is said that when the Buddha went back to meet his family after his enlightenment, he was given a stately welcome. His father, the king, treated him like the prince he once had been. The ministers and members of the royal family greeted him most reverentially. His own son, Rahula, ran up to him and hugged him tight. For seven years he had heard so much about his father, he had been waiting anxiously to see him. I continue the scene from *Yasodhara, the Wife of the Bodhisattva*[22] by Ranjini Obeyesekere:

> Yasodhara, the mother of Rahula, did not make an appearance.
>
> The king sent for Yasodhara, but she replied, 'Surely if I am deserving of any regard, Siddhartha will come and see me.'
>
> The Blessed One, having greeted all his relatives and friends, asked, 'Where is Yasodhara?'

And on being informed that she had refused to come, he rose straightaway and went to her apartments.

'I am free,' the Blessed One said to his disciples, Shariputra and Maudgalyayana whom he had bidden to accompany him to the princess's chamber. 'The princess however is not yet free. Not having seen me for a long time she is exceedingly sorrowful. Unless her grief is allowed its course her heart will cleave. Should she touch the Tathagata, the Holy One, you must not prevent her.'

Yasodhara sat in her room, dressed in mean garments and her hair cut. When the Buddha entered she was, from the abundance of her affection, like an overflowing vessel unable to contain her love. Forgetting that the man whom she loved was the Buddha, lord of the world, the preacher of truth, she held him by his feet and wept bitterly.

Remembering however that Suddhodana, the Shakya king and Buddha's father, was present she felt ashamed, and rising, seated herself reverently at a distance.

The king apologized for the princess saying, 'This arises from her deep affection and is more than a temporary emotion. During the seven years that she had lost her husband when she heard that Siddhartha had shaved his head, she did likewise; when she heard that he had left off the use of perfumes and ornaments, she also refused their use. Like her husband she had eaten at appointed times from an

> earthen bowl only. Like him she had renounced high beds and splendid coverings and when princes asked her hand in marriage she replied that she was still his. Therefore, grant her forgiveness.'

Most of our life's struggles are focused on avoiding grief and protecting happiness. If our expectations from life are met, we are happy, else we are sad. What makes our negative emotions even worse is our inability to correct them as soon as they arise. We feel helpless, we cry, we get angry, we don't want to, but we do. In the story I just quoted, two lines stand out in particular: 'Unless her grief is allowed its course her heart will cleave,' and, 'This arises from her deep affection and is more than a temporary emotion.'

The more vested we are in something or someone emotionally, the greater is our grief when things fall apart. As a river creates its own passage, grief runs its own course as well. You can map out the route of a river differently, but you can't stop it forever. Eventually, unless it dries up, it must merge in another river or in the sea. Grief, too, must be absorbed by a higher emotion or it never ebbs. Because, unlike most other emotions, grief is not a temporary or a fleeting feeling. It arises from the deepest point of love. The river of grief can only ever unite with the river of gratitude, it can only merge in the ocean of love. It hurts bad when a loved one exits from your life. And, until you are able to love someone else with the same intensity, you can't overcome your grief at the loss of the one you once had in your life.

Either you are lucky enough to find someone and love him/her with all your might or you learn to shift your attention; there aren't many other options of getting past your grief. It heals with time. Replace the source of grief or replenish yourself with love. At any rate, don't be sorry for grieving. After all, grief is not a choice but an emotion. Besides, it's futile to feel bad for feeling bad. It only makes you more contrite. Instead, when a certain emotion hits you, accept it and allow it to run its course. Allow the impact to wear off.

I must give a word of caution here: running its course does not mean that you contemplate it or worry about it. Thinking about your grief will, in fact, elongate the course. While you don't have to feel guilty for feeling sad, an attempt to gently shift your attention (to something positive or gratifying) should still be made. It will help you to gradually pull yourself and your mind out of it.

~

A disciple said to his master, 'I've an anger issue. I get really mad. What do I do?'

'Hmm…' said the master, stroking his white, flowing beard. 'I need to see your anger to understand its severity. Get angry for me now.' The disciple looked askance, and said, 'How can I show it to you right away? It's not like I can get angry anytime!'

'Oh,' the master said, 'if you can't show me your anger anytime you want that means it's not your true nature. Go to the source to harness it.'

Sadness and joy, like sorrow and happiness, spring from the same source – our mind. We feel them in our hearts, but they originate from the mind. Our emotions are like waves in the sea, ceaseless and inseparable. In the same ocean where you find priceless pearls and precious gems, you also find white sharks and killer whales. In the ocean of mind, in the sea of life, our feelings are constant, intricate and connected. It is impossible to always feel happy or be eternally sad. When we dive in our inner world, we are going to meet all forms of emotions.

Like creatures of the sea, our feelings, too, have a life of their own. Accept them to be at peace. The moment you are in harmony with all that you have in you, you naturally reach a tranquil state. And how could you be in harmony? Be mindful. Be grateful. Love and gratitude are the only terminal points of grief.

THE RIVER OF LIFE

If not us, who runs and controls our lives?

One day, Ma Shamata Om (my foremost disciple and one of the most graceful and beautiful souls I know) said something profound in her usual simple way.

'Swami,' she said, 'come to think of it, human life is so beautiful and simple. Get up every day, do good karma, eat a square meal, help others, serve humanity and get some rest. That's all there is. For some reason, most of us have made it too complex by too much thinking and worrying.'

Other than the message itself, the word that stood out for me was 'made'. In the act of making, we have come to see life as something we make. As if it's something we manufacture. The truth is we don't. There are only some aspects of it that we control but the rest, a vast majority, of the factors are completely free of our influence and preferences.

The moment we start seeing life as something we flow with as opposed to something we have to make, our perspective changes naturally. Unnecessary struggle takes a back seat and you become increasingly aware of where you need to surrender versus when you ought to take charge.

In a world driven by action and focused on results, we have placed too much emphasis on making. In *Let Your Life Speak,* Parker J. Palmer writes, 'If we lived close to nature in an agricultural society, the seasons as metaphor and fact would continually frame our lives. But the master metaphor of our era does not come from agriculture – it comes from manufacturing. We do not believe that we "grow" our lives – we believe that we "make" them. Just listen to how we use the word in everyday speech: we make time, make friends, make meaning, make money, make a living, make love.'

We don't make the oceans, mountains or the rivers. We don't make sunlight, clouds or the rain. We simply bear a witness to the majestic creation around us. Yogic texts state that each one of us has an entire universe within us. The Bible, too, says that the kingdom of God is within us. And, that kingdom, this universe of our inner world, has a whole range of places – from exquisitely beautiful to excruciatingly painful. There are dark woods of fear, marshes of negativity, rotting trees of ego, cacti of jealousy, creepers of covetousness, a quagmire of desires and a stinking residue of hate.

Having said that, in our same inner world there are some hauntingly beautiful places, too. An ocean of bliss, tides of love, seasons of life, the colours of spring, a phase of autumn, the warm winter sun of forgiveness, and beautiful moonless nights studded with stars of our random acts of kindness. It's all there. It's all here, in us, within us. In the journey of life, we have no other option but to pass through the various places. Where we choose to stay and for how long, whether we decide to inhabit a space for a short while or decide to make it our home, is our choice. But our life is not just about us, it's a much bigger phenomenon. A collective development, a cosmic process. Indeed, we are in life as much as life is in us.

Not all shades of life will appeal to us but they are there for a purpose. Sometimes, it helps to let Nature paint our canvas, to say to life 'take me where you want', to accept the wisdom of the Universe. We don't always have to burden ourselves to make things, to make them right or make them now. Sometimes, all we have to do is be patient and let go. At times, we must allow life to manifest the way it wants to.

> Some time when the river is ice ask me
> mistakes I have made. Ask me whether
> what I have done is my life. Others
> have come in their slow way into
> my thought, and some have tried to help
> or to hurt: ask me what difference
> their strongest love or hate has made.
>
> I will listen to what you say.
> You and I can turn and look
> at the silent river and wait. We know
> the current is there, hidden; and there

are comings and goings from miles away
that hold the stillness exactly before us.
What the river says, that is what I say.[23]

Surely, we want to be in control and lead our lives the way we prefer. But, if you ask me, the very idea of shaping is incomplete. We are not a piece of clay that needs moulding or a rock that requires sculpting. Maybe, we are just a gift from the Universe, a tiny seed that's waiting to be sprouted. Maybe, you just need a bit of nurturing, a bit of care and you'll emerge as a tender sapling first, and later, a giant tree laden with fruits of love and kindness. After all, everything is already there in you, just waiting to be discovered.

The river of life flows independently of one's preferences. Whether you flow, float, swim or sink, it's your personal choice.

THE LAST LETTER

When the day arrives, in the final analysis, what will be on your mind?

In any given year, on average, I skim over 10,000 emails, and 3000+ notes and letters sent to me physically during various events. This does not include hundreds of group and personal meetings, and just as many questions I read and answer in Swaminars. There's also my work. Black Lotus, my blog, the ashram, writing, editors, publishers, travel, events, and so on. In other words, a large part of my time goes in interacting with people.

Even with the constant barrage of emails and issues that demand my attention, somehow, her note had caught my eye. She first wrote to my admin team four years ago and I agreed to meet her instantly. She was not in a position to travel to the ashram, so we made arrangements to see her during one of my stopovers.

A frail, beautiful soul, Vandana Sharma, just over forty summers old, had both a bit of fear and hope in her eyes when I met her three years ago. She had been fighting cancer since 2015. It was at an advanced stage and had metastasized already. She wanted to be well again and live, she told me in no uncertain terms, and Vandana was deeply worried about her young children. Never-ending treatments in the form of surgeries, medication, chemo, and radiation had wreaked havoc on her well-being.

At times, she had no energy to walk. She had been brought to me in a wheelchair. But she would always be just as smiling and nervous as any other time.

She had come to me with a lot of faith, but how could I promise her something that was no longer in my hands? Could I? Did I? No.

And yet, I continued to see Vandana with her family and her ever-loving husband by her side. Whenever I could manage, I set aside a few minutes to see her and I must have met her five times or so. She sensed early on that I would not be able to grant her wish. I knew I could not do anything to help her stay on a bit longer in this planet. She had been handed an eviction notice by Mother Nature. Perhaps, a truer way to say it would be that she was being transferred. She had served her time here and I could not get her an extension.

Then, on Guru Poornima (16 July 2019), her husband visited me. Like every other time, he had handmade laddoos for me. Two boxes. One small one, I kept, and the other, I blessed and returned. This had been our tradition since the very first meeting. We both knew that I didn't really consume sweets, but that was immaterial.

He gave me an envelope, and said, 'Vandana wanted you to have this letter. I discovered it after her passing.'

I waited until the event was over because I wanted to read it in peace. It sat on my table for three days, in plain sight, reminding me that I had to give it the time and attention it deserved. I share it with you literatim, with the consent and permission of her husband. I have retained the paragraphing, punctuation and syntax exactly the way Vandana (17 May 1974–6 May 2019) wrote.

Swamiji
Shat-shat Pranam.

If you are reading this then we both know what that means.

No problem!

I'm so grateful to almighty for bringing you in my life at the time when I needed a guru to get me through the last and most difficult phase of my life. I'm going with a calm and peaceful heart and mind.

I'm sad but not scared. Sad because of the emotional attachments but not scared of what is to come. This evolution is only because of you.

I don't know if I have changed but I feel and think differently now. I'm in immense pain but still I'm not angry with my circumstances, life or God. I've realised that I'm the creator of all my sufferings. All I have is deep love for every person I ever met. They are all me.

There was a time when I had energy and life but no idea what to do with it and now when I've gained a pinch of wisdom, there is no energy or life left. I wish I could get a chance to put it to good use with the right intent. That's my only regret.

I used to worry a lot about my kids and especially [my husband]. He is my soulmate and his world revolves around me but I'm not worried anymore because I know you are there to take care of all of them.

I used to wonder that if god had to give me life till now only then why not just take me through in a second with a stroke or accident! Why put me through this torture for more than 4 years? Now I understand the complete overhauling my soul has undergone to emerge more evolved.

It's a small price I paid.

I have a small request.

In all my lifetimes henceforth no matter what life form or vessel I will take on, just keep me around you in some or the other way. I don't know how much my soul has wandered in search of your grace but now that I've found you I want to be just under its blessings. I know all my relations and attachments will keep changing in each lifetime but this one connect I want to continue till eternity. Promise me you will keep me around you always in every lifetime.

With a very certain belief that we will meet very soon I'm saying goodbye to you.

You are my guru, my love, my god.

Thank you for all your unconditional love and support.

I might not recognise you but I'm sure you will find me.

Jai Shri Hari

Vandana

Tathastu, I say.

The letter itself is the message I have for you today. Please know that one day it's going to come to an end. Live your life like you love it and care for it. We really don't have the time to spend on petty thoughts, emotions, grudges, resentment, negativity. And, if you think you do, think again.

Make up or move on.

And yes, Vandana, Om Swami will find you. Like I've kept my word to the ones I've found (ongoing) this time around, Swami will find you. It's my job, my dharma, neither of which I take for granted.

NOTES

1 SN stands for Samyutta Nikaya.

2 Brahm, Ajahn. *Bear Awareness: Questions and Answers on Taming Your Wild Mind*. Wisdom Publications, 2017.

3 Viharas were often places where the Buddha stopped by during various times of the year and spent time either discoursing or in solitude. 'Vihara' is a Sanskrit word that usually means to take a leisurely stroll. His devotees built these viharas for him so the Buddha could rest and recuperate. Later, these were the places where monks congregated and eventually became monasteries.

4 Caplow, Zenshin Florence, and Reigetsu Susan Moon (eds). *The Hidden Lamp: Stories from Twenty-Five Centuries of Awakened Women*. Wisdom Publications, 2013.

5 Prabhupada, A.C. Bhaktivedanta Swami. *Srimad Bhagavatam, Eleventh Canto*. The Bhaktivedanta Book Trust, 2012.

6 Frankl, Viktor E. *Man's Search for Meaning*. Beacon Press, 1992.

7 Asimov, Isaac. *Isaac Asimov's Treasury of Humor: 640 Jokes, Anecdotes, and Limericks, Complete with Notes on How to Tell Them*. Mariner Books, 1991.

8 Buber, Martin. *Tales of the Hasidim*. Schocken, 1991.

9 Palmer, Parker J. *Let Your Life Speak: Listening for the Voice of Vocation*. Jossey-Bass, 2009.

10 Haig, Matt. *Notes on a Nervous Planet*. Canongate Books, 2018.

11 This story appears in Jeffrey Davis, *1,000 Marbles: A Little Something about Precious Time,* Kansas City: Andrews McMeel Publishing, 2001, pp. xi–xiv. https://bit.ly/2PsQGFB

12 Hanh, Thich Nhat. *Being Peace*. Parallax Press, 2005.

13 Shankarananda, Swami. *The Yoga of Kashmir Shaivism: Consciousness is Everything*. Motilal Banarsidass, 2016.

14 Merton, Thomas. *The Way of Chuang Tzu*. New Directions, 2010.

15 Taleb, Nassim Nicholas. *The Bed of Procrustes: Philosophical and Practical Aphorisms*. Random House, 2016.

16 Becker, Laney Katz. *Three Times Chai: 54 Rabbis Tell Their Favorite Stories*. Behrman House, 2007.

17 Kranc, Moshe. *The Hasidic Masters' Guide to Management*. Devora Publishing, 2004.

18 Adyashanti. 'Selling Water by the River'. In *Inner Directions Journal*, Fall/Winter 1999.

19 Laxman, R.K. *The Distorted Mirror: Stories, Travelogues, Sketches*. Penguin India, 2004.

20 Hanh, Thich Nhat. *Thich Nhat Hanh: Essential Writings*. Orbis Books, 2001.

21 Masters, Jarvis Jay. *Finding Freedom: Writings from Death Row*. Padma Pub, 1997.

22 Obeyesekere, Ranjini. *Yasodharā, the Wife of the Bōdhisattva: The Sinhala* Yasodharāvatā *(The Story of Yasodharā) and the Sinhala* Yasodharāpadānaya *(The Sacred Biography of Yasodharā)*. State University of New York Press, 2009.

23 Stafford, William. *Ask Me: 100 Essential Poems of William Stafford*. Graywolf Press, 2013.

ABOUT THE AUTHOR

Om Swami is a mystic who lives in the Himalayan foothills. Prior to renunciation, he founded and ran a multimillion-dollar software company with offices across the world. He is also the author of the bestselling books *If Truth be Told: A Monk's Memoir* (HarperCollins, 2014), *The Wellness Sense: A Practical Guide to Your Physical and Emotional Health Based on Ayurvedic and Yogic Wisdom* (HarperCollins, 2015), *When All Is Not Well: Depression, Sadness and Healing – A Yogic Perspective* (HarperCollins, 2016), *The Last Gambit* (HarperCollins, 2017), *Mind Full to Mindful: Zen Wisdom from a Monk's Bowl* (HarperCollins, 2018), *The Children of Tomorrow: A Monk's Guide to Mindful Parenting* (HarperCollins, 2019) and *The Book of Kindness: How to Make Others Happy and Be Happy Yourself* (HarperCollins, 2019).

Made in the USA
Monee, IL
26 May 2023

34597668R00121